Giovanna

Giovanna

◆

Angels in Hell

A True Story of a Jewish-Italian Child's Survival of WWII

Sylvia Smith Skrmetta

iUniverse, Inc.

New York Lincoln Shanghai

Giovanna
Angels in Hell

iUniverse books may be ordered through booksellers or by contacting:

iUniverse
2021 Pine Lake Road, Suite 100
Lincoln, NE 68512
www.iuniverse.com
1-800-Authors (1-800-288-4677)

ISBN-13: 978-0-595-39981-9 (pbk)
ISBN-13: 978-0-595-84369-5 (ebk)
ISBN-10: 0-595-39981-9 (pbk)
ISBN-10: 0-595-84369-7 (ebk)

Printed in the United States of America

For my mother

Contents

Preface xiii

Timeline xv

Part I   *Tripoli*

CHAPTER 1 3

CHAPTER 2 6

CHAPTER 3 12

CHAPTER 4 16

CHAPTER 5 19

CHAPTER 6 21

CHAPTER 7 23

Part II   *Italy WWII*

CHAPTER 8 29

CHAPTER 9 32

CHAPTER 10 35

CHAPTER 11. 38

CHAPTER 12 41

CHAPTER 13 45

CHAPTER 14 48

CHAPTER 15 52

CHAPTER 16 55

CHAPTER 17 59

CHAPTER 18 61

CHAPTER 19 65

CHAPTER 20 68

CHAPTER 21 70

CHAPTER 22 73

CHAPTER 23 77

CHAPTER 24 79

CHAPTER 25 81

CHAPTER 26 84

Part III   Return to Tripoli

CHAPTER 27 89

CHAPTER 28 93

CHAPTER 29 97

CHAPTER 30 99

CHAPTER 31 101

CHAPTER 32 103

CHAPTER 33 106

CHAPTER 34 109

CHAPTER 35 111

CHAPTER 36 113

CHAPTER 37 116

CHAPTER 38 119
Epilogue 127

Author's Note 133

Acknowledgements

I believe nothing is accomplished totally alone. Therefore, I would like to thank my husband Jimmy Skrmetta, my daughters, Brandie Spradley, Christy Strong, and Jamie Parolli for their unending support of all my creative endeavors.

To my father, Ford Smith, thank you Dad for the photographs and memories you added to this story and for loving my mother for all these years.

I would also like to thank my brother David Smith for his photographs of the convent in Florence, my brothers Benny Smith and Bruce Smith for allowing me to accompany them to Florence and the Trentino Region to see first hand the places my mother had been in the war, and a huge thank you to my brother Victor Smith for his stunning cover concept.

My gratitude to my friends and family who assisted with the editing of my manuscript, and most importantly, thank you mom for allowing me to share your story with the world.

Preface

"Even when the bombs were falling all around us, I was never afraid! You see, I was just a child—like you are right now. I didn't think anything could hurt me! Some of the other children were afraid and cried. The younger children screamed for their mothers, but of course, our mothers and fathers were very far away from us." As the elderly woman spoke, sadness seemed to creep into her eyes for just a moment as she stepped back in time. She quickly turned her attention back to the class of young children and their teachers who seemed eager for her to continue her story.

She was no taller than a fifth-grader, petite in stature, and her boyish-cut hair had only a hint of gray. She was neatly dressed in a casual suit, and she wore brown leather shoes on her tiny feet. On her right wrist, seven gold bangle bracelets chimed in unison as she moved her arms. The dark-rimmed glasses seemed too large for her face, and through the bifocal lenses, her dark brown eyes still danced with the energy she had within her. As she addressed the children, she smiled, revealing nearly perfect white teeth.

Except for the occasional comment from a student about how small the lady was, the young audience was silent when she began to speak. Her charm and charisma were apparent from the moment she uttered her first words. "My name is Giovanna Bonifazio Smith," she began. "I am of Jewish-Italian descent. I was asked to come to your school today to tell you a little about my life, my country, and World War II." Except for the noticeable Italian accent, she spoke perfect English.

I listened to my seventy-four-year-old mother tell her story. It unfolded in perfect chronological order. Perhaps the children found some bit of information about the war they might retell or use in their reports, but on that day I found my mother.

For fifty-four years of my life, I had only heard bits and pieces of the drama she was now sharing with all of us in that room. I realized there was so much more to this woman, and I was ashamed I had never taken the time to ask her about her life. I had accepted the crumbs she had offered and had left it at that. Now I hungered for more than crumbs; I wanted the entire cake. I wanted to know all the ingredients that had formed the woman in front of me.

For nearly two years, I prompted my mother for any information about her life during WWII. At first, she had difficulty remembering the details I wanted from her. Some memories were so painful that we both cried. Eventually, I had her mind working night and day. Many mornings my mother would call me to say she had remembered something while she was sleeping—even in her dreams she was reaching into the past. This is her story, as it she told it to me, of love, family, and war.

Timeline

1913   Silvestro Bonifazio immigrates to Tripoli, Libya.

1927   The marriage of Silvestro Bonifazio to Camilla Fargion.

1929   The birth of Giovanna, October 26.

1932   The birth of Enrico.

1936   Silvestro Bonifazio declares bankruptcy.

1937   The birth of Guido, August.

1938   The death of Enrico.
        Camilla hospitalized.

1939   The death of Silvestro Bonifazio, November.

1940   Giovanna sent to Italy, June 10.
        British air raids begin on Naples, November.

1941   Giovanna and Guido baptized and confirmed into the Catholic Church.

1942   Females from Arenella convent sent to Rovereto.

1943   Giovanna sent to the convent in Florence.
        German soldiers and Italian Secret Service invade the convent, November.
        Eighty Jewish women and children arrested and sent to Auschwitz.

1944   Allied occupation of Florence, August.

1945   Mussolini hung, April.
        Giovanna goes to Bologna.

1946   Giovanna returns to Naples.

1947   Camilla sails to Naples, January.
        Giovanna and Guido return to Tripoli, March.

1948   Giovanna and Ford meet, January.

1949   The marriage of Giovanna Bonifazio to Ford Smith, May 7.

PART I
Tripoli

1

They said Mussolini was a good man; at least, that is what most people said. My father was anti-fascist, not fond of any party, especially Mussolini's. *Il Duce* (the leader), as he was called, had built schools all over Italy. People from depressed regions of our homeland could find work and property through his economic efforts—surely only a good man would do such a thing. I for one was oblivious to the man, his politics, and the political drama that was unfolding in Europe. My youthfulness spared me the realization that my fellow classmates and I were dressed identically, the boys in their Balilla uniforms, and the girls in their smocks. I was unaware that our schoolwork, from the colored Fascist illustrations and quotations, to photographs of Mussolini and quotations from his frequent speeches, was tailored in every possible way to influence our young minds and spirits. Every day, without fail, I stood at attention with my fellow classmates, all of us dressed in our required uniforms, and pledged allegiance to the party and its leader.

Perhaps, Mussolini's colonization effort in North Africa was the only policy of *Il Duce* that met with my father's approval. In his efforts to make Italy a great power, Mussolini endeavored to increase his empire by creating Italian colonies in foreign lands. Many Italians were swayed to new countries by being given a house and a small plot of land to farm. Grape vineyards and olive trees grew from the toil of the farmers in this new land. The farmers sold their goods to vendors, who in turn peddled the fruit, vegetables, eggs, and olive oil through the city streets from wooden carts. The bellowing of the vendor as he yelled *"uove...olio"* ("eggs-oil") brought out the busy housewives and housekeepers to purchase his goods.

The Mediterranean Sea held a bounty for fishermen as well. Fish as large as tuna to the smallest sardine were pulled from the sea and sold in the fish markets and from wooden carts.

In 1913, two years after the Italian occupation of Libya, my father went to Tripoli to expand his business to the new Italian settlement. He and his partner, a Jewish man by the name of Cohen, were in the linen exporting business and supplied fine Italian linens throughout Tripoli and neighboring North African cities.

The Jewish community accounted for nearly a quarter of the population of Tripoli, and in the early days of the Italian occupation the Jewish people made great strides along side of their new neighbors. My father made many friends and acquaintances through his business travels. He became familiar with the Arabic and Jewish cultures as he conducted business in North Africa, but it was through his business partner that my father met my Jewish mother, Camilla Fargion.

It must have been difficult for my mother to marry an older man who was widowed with children from his previous marriage, and of a different faith. I would think that she must have considered that Silvestro Bonifazio was a man of means and could keep her financially and socially secure. Regretfully, I never had the opportunity to talk with my mother about those things. I only knew that despite the age and religious differences, my mother accepted Silvestro's marriage proposal.

For their marriage to be blessed and recognized by the Roman Catholic Church, Camilla would have had to abandon her own faith to become a convert. Her religious beliefs stemmed from hundreds of years of Jewish ancestry. Her own grandfather had been a Rabbi and a scholar, and she was deeply rooted in her Jewish faith. She refused to become Catholic. My father must have been totally in love and willing to do whatever it took to marry Camilla.

I was told many times by my Jewish relatives that seven Jewish Rabbi were present at my father's circumcision, for there would be no marriage until this was done. They were married in the synagogue and again in front of a judge.

At the time of my birth, the Catholic Church did not recognize my parents' civil marriage, and for a time, I was given my mother's last name of Fargion. A few months after my birth, Italian legislation changed, and non-Catholic marriages were recognized by the church. My father was finally able to give my mother and me his last name.

Tripoli, Libya

2

My story begins with my birth on October 26, 1929 in the Italian colony in Tripoli, Libya. The city was known as "The Jewel of the Mediterranean." Although just outside the city were vast stretches of sand and the rolling dunes of the Sahara Desert, the city itself enjoyed a Mediterranean climate. Evidence of the ancient Roman civilization that once occupied parts of this region left its mark on the city's buildings and roads.

Palm and date trees lined the streets and avenues of the beautiful city that embraced the sea. Marble sculptures adorned the centers of fountains that had been fashioned after the magnificent masterpieces of Italy. A few automobiles, many motorcycles and bicycles, and horse-drawn carriages provided transportation within the city. Camels and donkeys remained a common site outside the city and in the desert. Sometimes, if one were fortunate, you could gaze upon the magnificence of the Arabian horses.

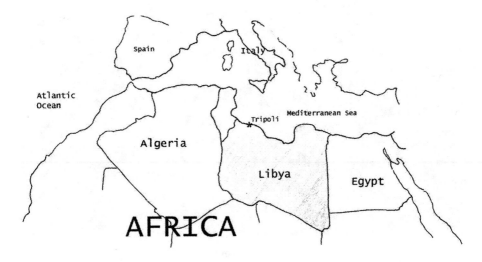

I was named Giovanna Vittoria Iris Bonifazio. My father, Silvestro Francesco Bonifazio, *Don Ciccio* to his friends, was born in Catania, Sicily, and my mother, Camilla Fargion, was from Tripoli. Although there was a twenty-five-year difference in age between my parents, *Don Ciccio* fathered three children with his new wife—my brothers Enrico, Guido, and me.

Papa was the best looking man in the world to me. I was crazy about him. Although he wasn't very tall, he had a commanding presence that kept me in awe. Everyday when he went to work he wore a tailor-made suit complete with a vest, and he donned his very handsome felt hat.

In the evenings, I would wait for my father to return home to partake of our daily ritual. I waited patiently, peaking out of the door or window to look for his arrival. My eagerness was apparent as I paced and watched for him. "Giovanna," my mother would say, "be patient my daughter. He will be here soon." The moment I heard his automobile or spotted him in the distance, my heart began to pound.

My father knew I was waiting for him and would look for me as soon as he got out of his automobile. His smile and outstretched arms were worth my agonizing wait. Once in the house, he would pick me up, hold me close to him, and give me a huge kiss on my cheek. "What have you been doing today *Piccola* (little one). Have you been a good girl? Have you obeyed your mother?"

"Oh yes Papa," I would assure him as he sat down in his favorite blue velvet chair. "I have been very good!"

He would cradle me on his lap as if he had been gone a long time. As he smiled, only his bottom lip showed beneath his thick bushy mustache. His blue eyes were filled with joy as I rubbed the top of his bald head, pulled at his coarse gray mustache, and demanded my daily surprise. I stuck my tiny hand in every pocket of his vest until I found my gift. It never mattered to me if the surprise was a piece of candy or a small trinket; it was the game with my father that was important to me.

Sometimes, as Papa would nod off to sleep, I would remain on his lap, and I would play with his gold watch and chain that was always tucked safely away in his lower right vest pocket. Other times he would sit with me until I had exhausted all the questions I had managed to think of during his absence. I could ask him a thousand questions, and he would have answered them all.

My mother was always amazed at the political discussions my father and I would have after listening to some bit of news on the radio. *"Ciccio,"* as she called my father, *"cosa fai? E' una bambina!"* ("What are you doing? She is a little girl!")

"Lei vuol sapere!" ("She wants to know!") My father responded.

Mama would walk away shaking her head from side to side in total helplessness. She often reverted to speaking Hebrew when she encountered her husband's stubbornness and her daughter's inquisitive mind. Camilla was already in acceptance of the fact that Giovanna was not a typical little girl.

Playing with dolls or dressing up in their mothers' dresses were favorite pastimes for my female cousins, but not for me. Mama tried. Once she bought me a beautiful porcelain doll that was taller than I was by several inches. The doll had sparkling blue eyes with eyelids that opened and shut. It also cried out "ma-ma" when I tilted her over. I stared at that doll for hours, trying to figure out the mechanisms that would allow this toy to do such marvelous things. Within hours, I took the expensive doll apart to reveal her secrets. Except for the wooden Pinocchio that I had gotten as a baby, I don't remember getting anymore dolls after my porcelain victim.

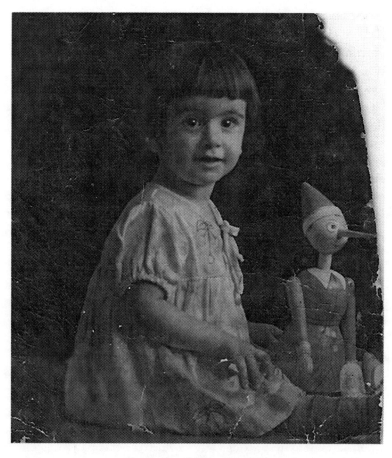

Giovanna and Pinocchio 1930

Maybe my closeness to my father stemmed in part from his acceptance of my curiosity, and his willingness to overlook my gender and give me the same mental stimulation usually reserved for males. There never seemed to be an end to his patience with me or my brothers when they came along to push me off his lap.

Papa read constantly and was always abreast of the world news. One day as we were listening to the radio, Papa pointed to the speaker in the center and said, "Giovanna, do you see this place in the center of the radio?"

I was looking intensely at the radio as he spoke. "Yes, Papa, I see it. That is where the voices come through."

"Yes, that is right, but one day soon we will be able to see real moving pictures of people in that same spot!"

I stared at my father in awe. "How do you know this Papa?"

"Mr. Marconi told me himself," he stated.

"Do you mean <u>the</u> Mr. Marconi?"

"I met him on one of my business trips to Italy. Such an intelligent man! He has done a lot of very important work."

I couldn't believe what I was hearing—first, that my father knew such an important man, the inventor of the wireless telegraph, and then, that there would be little people in my radio one day! His statement just reinforced my belief that my father was a very important and brilliant man himself. It was not everyone who could meet and converse with the famous Guglielmo Marconi! "And," I thought to myself, "I am the daughter of the very important *Signor* Silvestro Bonifazio! Huh! Not every little girl could say that either!"

Papa was very good at spending time with all of his and Camilla's children. Many times I watched him and my little brother Enrico sit side by side on the sofa, each with a page of the newspaper in front of his face. Papa would glance down at his little boy who was desperately trying to hold up the flimsy page that was nearly as large as he was, and he would smile. At first, *Ricco*, as the family called him, pretended to read. Then one day as he struggled with the newspaper page, he asked Papa about a headline. "What does it mean, Papa?" he asked quite seriously.

Papa looked over and nearly dropped his own paper. My father called out to my mother, "Camilla, come quickly!" My mother, startled by the urgency in my father's voice, came running from the kitchen where she had been busily preparing our evening meal.

"Che cosa Ciccio?" ("What is it?") She asked as she surveyed the room.

"Guarda, guarda," ("Look, look") he said excitedly. "Look at what your son can do!"

Ricco seemed surprised at the sudden outbreak. *"Mamma,"* he stated with all sincerity, "I only wanted Papa to explain what they meant in this story." My parents looked at each other in total bewilderment. *Ricco* had read the headline, and he had not yet reached the age of five.

One of Papa's favorite reading places was his blue velvet chair. The chair was positioned under the crystal chandelier in the sitting room, and at an angle that made it possible for him to see the big Swiss clock that hung on the wall behind the sofa.

I loved to watch my father read. Often, as he read, he would play one of his many opera recordings on his gramophone. The gramophone always amazed me. This uncomplicated looking box had a rather large cylinder with a flared opening that was able to produce the most beautiful sounds! How amazing! On the cylinder were the words *"La Voce Del Padrone"* (The Master's Voice) and a drawing of a dog listening to a gramophone. Of course, my father had to explain this phenomenon to me.

Sometimes Papa would look up from his reading material (probably sensing I was bored or needed his attention), his blue eyes sparkled through the little round lenses of his black metal-framed glasses, and he would smile at me the same way he had smiled at *Ricco*. "Shall we catch the chameleons, *Piccola?*" He would put down his book, take me by the hand, and together we began our nightly search for his pet chameleons that he had let loose during the day. Their ability to change color to hide from their pursuer was futile—my father knew just where to look for the scaly creatures. After catching them, he would put them back in their cage for the night. Besides our family, the servants, the chameleons, turtles, and canaries shared our palace, along with an occasional uninvited desert guest, the scorpion.

Silvestro Bonifazio (Papa) 1932

3

My mother was born in 1903 and was twenty-six-years-old when I was born. The Fargions originated from Holland and were of the Jewish faith with Spanish ancestry. Camilla was tall and thin, with hair so black that it seemed blue. Except for a small photograph of her taken a few months before her death, my memories of her face are gone. The beauty I seem to remember from my childhood was replaced with the haunting image of the frail and sickly face of a woman I never got to know.

Mama believed in being properly dressed and in displaying proper etiquette at all times. It was these things she drilled into her children. She and my father were very diligent in teaching proper table manners, speech, and conduct to their children, especially in the presence of adults. I was always to conduct myself as a young lady should—with no exceptions. Camilla would not tolerate any of her children interrupting an adult conversation. The punishment did not stop me from voicing my opinion in an adult conversation, and I was often sent to my room for my rudeness. I am sure Mama blamed her husband for allowing me to express my views with him in our frequent discussions.

My father was more innovative with his corrections. Table manners were drilled into our heads from the time we were able to sit for a meal. As a rule, Italians do not put their elbows on the table at any time during a meal. However, one may rest their wrists on the edge of the tabletop without compromising etiquette. One day I made the dreadful mistake of having my elbows on top of the table (and probably giving my opinion freely at dinner). My father said nothing. Instead, he slowly walked behind me, grabbed my forearms, pulled them straight up in the air, and then slammed them down on the table. I screamed out like a yelping dog. That's the day I discovered my "funny-bone" (which wasn't at all funny), and I learned never to make that mistake again!

As a young girl, I suffered from anemia. Perhaps I was so busy with questions, discoveries of the world, and playing, that I had little interest in food. At any rate, my mother's cure, which I doubt she thought of herself, was a steak that came from a horse. Horsemeat, according to my mother, had much more iron than beef. Mama would sit me at the kitchen table, put the slice of meat on my plate, and say, "Eat!"

As small as I was, my eyes were almost level with the tabletop and the plate. The meat seemed to stare at me as its hot juices seeped down on the plate. *"Ma e' cavallo!"* ("But it's a horse!") I cried.

My mother, realizing she had made a huge mistake in telling me what I was eating, tried a different approach. "Did I say horse? No, no! I meant cow!"

I was not to be fooled, but I was not going to win a battle against my mother. I finally took a bite. I immediately knew this was no cow! The meat was tough and chewy. I gagged, but managed to eat a small portion of the "iron wonder!" After that day, I made more of an effort to eat my meals. Of course, being threatened with another horse steak enticed me to eat whatever else my mother put on my plate!

Unlike my father, my mother was on the nervous side. My father, for the most part, seemed calm—nothing seemed to bother him. He was happy with Camilla and his new family. My mother seemed happy to me, but my memory of her during those days is shadowed by all the events that followed. She remained strong in her faith and was a very good and generous woman who gave of her time to needy families.

On Fridays before sunset, she would bring these families a *coffa* (basket) of food for their Sabbath meal. It would not have surprised me if my mother had offered her good deeds to God in exchange for His blessings on our family.

I looked forward to the Sabbath, the twenty-four hour period that fell from Friday at sundown to Saturday at sundown. To my mother, as well as her relatives, this was a time of rest and spiritual enrichment. For me though, it was much more than that. I was neither Catholic nor Jewish by laws of either faith, although many of my aunts insisted I was Jewish by being born to a Jewish mother. While my Jewish relatives could not work, turn on or off lights, handle money, cook, or partake of any of the activities in the long list of restrictions of the Sabbath, I was not bound by any of those things. Therefore, I was an eagerly invited guest to my Jewish relatives' homes. Of course, it was fun to be able to play with my cousins, but because I was under no restrictions, I could do things for them around the house that they could not. With me in their homes, my relatives could enjoy warmed food and lights. I was allowing them the conveniences without compromising their Sabbath.

Even though I enjoyed being their helper and playing with my cousins, it was the chance to go to the cinema every weekend that really drove me to badgering my mother to allow me to go and stay with my relatives during the Sabbath. Because my relatives could not touch or handle money during this time of the week, they would have me pick up the money from the dresser in their home and pay for our tickets into the cinema house.

My mother enjoyed going to her relatives for the gathering and blessing of the family, but she celebrated the Sabbath at home much of the time. When she did remain home for the celebration, she did not take advantage of my Catholic father. All of her meals were cooked before sundown on Friday, and she preset our table with a fine white linen table cloth, our best china, flowers, and candles which my father would light. Her servants returned to their homes, many times with baskets of food my mother had prepared for them. Although my father never drank wine or beer, my mother enjoyed wine with her meal, and she allowed me to drink water with a few spoons of wine added for color. We all ate of the *challah* (loaf of twisted bread), and our plates were filled with Jewish, Italian, or Arabic foods that had been lovingly prepared for us.

Our servants respected and loved my mother. Besides the baskets of food she gave them on the Sabbath, she often found the time to help them and their families with their problems.

Among our servants, we had an Arab youth who might have been seventeen or eighteen years old. My parents called him our "house-boy." Beside the many errands he ran for my father and mother, one of his many duties was to take me to the park each day. To me it seemed that he enjoyed this time as much as I did, perhaps even more so. He is one of my happy memories. After hours of running and playing in the park, to both of our dismay, it would be time to return home. Without fail, I would complain of how very tired I was, and that I couldn't possibly make it home on my own two feet. He would smile and lift me in his arms. I would immediately rest my head on his shoulder, dangle my limp arms, and pretend to fall asleep. Once we arrived at home, he gently handed me over to my parents who had long become accustomed to my charade, and he would say, "The poor girl is so tired; she probably needs to be put in her bed." That was my cue to make a remarkable recovery from my state of slumber!

I loved him and thought of him as my friend. And he in turn, seemed to love me and my family as well. Having him, as well as the other servants as part of my life, helped me to learn and to understand Arabic and Hebrew.

Then one day, the unthinkable happened. Shortly after the Arab youth had gone back to his own home, one of his relatives came running to our *palazzina* (little palace). She was screaming for my mother to help her. My mother did not hesitate. She ran out of the door and followed the boy's relative to his home. There she found the young man's lifeless body on a small cot on the floor. He had been stung by a scorpion and had died before my mother could get to him. It was a sad day, one I shall always remember.

4

Although I was very young, I seemed to understand that our way of life was much better than most people we knew. It was the life I knew then—the *palazzina*, chauffeur driven cars, and servants. It was my birthright and I was unaware that my life could ever change.

The *palazzina* had a double-garage (unheard of in those days) that housed our four cars. One of the cars was a Fiat Balilla with a tag that bore my name. My father had promised the Balilla to me when I grew up. "One day I shall teach you to drive the Balilla, *Piccola,* and then you can drive me around the city. Would you like that?" He would pick me up and swing me around and around.

"Oh yes, Papa!" I squealed in pure delight, "I will drive you anywhere you want to go! I shall drive Mama too! When can I learn Papa? When?"

"Soon, Giovanna, very soon," he would say, and I believed him.

The *palazzina* was situated in the heart of the city and on the same street as the Governor's palace. It was very beautiful with huge rooms, high ceilings, marble floors, thick hand-made rugs woven by Arab artisans, crystal chandeliers, and a long elegant stairway with a fine mahogany handrail that graced the path to the second story. At the top of the stairs was a beautifully ornate wooden door. It seemed perfect and lavish—much like my image of our family. The stained glass that adorned the center of the door reflected the colors of the rainbow. Many times I gazed at the sun's rays bouncing off of the glass causing a wondrous display of colors on the wall. It is not surprising to me that I remember that door. It was at the top of the stairs, near this door, that my first bout with fear and uneasiness overcame me.

My father and his first wife had four children before her death. These sons and daughters of my father were much older than the children he had with Camilla. I only had the opportunity to get close to Renzo, his youngest son. Although he was considerably older than *Ricco* and me, he seemed to accept my father's marriage to Camilla and he loved his new siblings.

Peppino (short for Giuseppe), another of my father's sons, was a different story. He seemed to resent the marriage and did not disguise his dislike for my mother or want anything to do with her children.

Peppino was very handsome. Even as a little girl I would admire his good looks, but I thought he paled in comparison to my stepbrother Renzo, or for that matter, my beloved father.

My half-brother's lifestyle invited trouble for him and our family. He was a renowned gambler who enjoyed betting on race cars, motorcycles, and horses. He was a married man with a family, but was often seen in the company of other women.

When Peppino's debts became too large for him to pay, he went to my father. Being the loving person that he was, my father would help him—over and over again. I am not sure if perhaps Peppino's life was in danger from the debts, but I know my father did not turn his son down.

It was at the top of our stairs by the glass door when I heard Mama and Peppino arguing. This was not the first time I had witnessed the exchange of unpleasant words, but it would be the last.

My mother was trying to talk some sense into Peppino's head. "Can't you see what you are doing to your father? Why do you do these things?" she screamed as he was going into the house.

Immediately he turned to her, all the rage and frustration that he had within him burst in a moment of fury. "Get away from me you Jewish hag!" He pushed my mother with all his strength, causing her to tumble backward. She grabbed the mahogany handrail just before the impending fall.

My father, having heard the screams, came running to my mother. *"Dio mio, Dio mio!"* ("My God! My God!") He yelled. "Peppino, what have you done?" Papa gently embraced my sobbing mother and helped her up the stairs while Peppino tried feverishly to explain what had happened. Papa said nothing until after he had mama safely in the house, then he turned to face his son. "Leave and never show your face in my house again."

I had never seen this side of my father. His face had turned blood red, his voice was low and threatening, and his eyes seemed like steel daggers. Within seconds, the look of pain replaced that of anger as my father turned away from his son for the last time.

According to my mother, my father's eventual bankruptcy was caused by his vain attempts to save his misguided son. The gambling debts, attorney fees, and the debts incurred by the numerous cars and motorbikes Peppino had destroyed finally brought my father to ruin. I think the loss of his fortune was nothing in comparison to the heartbreak his son had caused him.

After depleting my father's resources, Peppino went to Ethiopia on a new venture—he opened a cinema in the country Mussolini's army had attacked and occupied. I was told by my mother that Peppino was taken prisoner and sent to a concentration camp. I never knew why. His repeated attempts to escape eventually led to his execution.

5

The bankruptcy was not enough to break my father's spirit, but my mother must have sensed the beginning of the end of life as we knew it. We lost the *palazzina* and most of our beautiful possessions. In a fit of despair, my distraught mother broke the stained glass in the door at the top of the stairs. It shattered into a thousand tiny pieces; only a hollow door remained where beauty and richness once prevailed.

The new rented house was not bad, nothing like our little palace, but comfortable enough for our new life's status. My father managed to open a small grocery store near our new home. We no longer owned any of our cars, and Papa was forced to walk to work each day. I never heard him complain.

On his way home, he would stop at the bakery to buy a loaf of freshly baked bread. Sometimes it would still be warm from the ovens. He often walked home slowly, his hands clutching the bread behind his back, and his mind a thousand miles away. When he arrived home, he handed the bread to my mother as if it was a bouquet of flowers, and she accepted the bread with as much gratitude.

It was not unusual for me to go with my father to his grocery store. I had convinced myself that I was his assistant and would sit on the counter to wait for his customers to come into the store. I greeted the customers with a very cheerful *"buon giorno,"* ("good day") and I would ask how could I help them. This always brought a chuckle and comments to *Don Ciccio* about his young helper. But my real pleasure came when children accompanied their relatives into the store. I then freely, and at my father's expense, gave out candy—lots of candy! The kind-hearted grocer only laughed as his little daughter generously treated the neighborhood children. The more candy I gave away, the more children came into the store. My charitable nature was undoubtedly acquired from both my parents. I believe my father would have given food away if it were not for the fact he had his own family to feed. It was his kind heart that led him to accept credit instead of payment from many of his less fortunate customers. Soon he became unable to keep the grocery store open and was forced to seek employment elsewhere.

It was in the new house that my youngest brother Guido was born. I was lying in my bed that day, blankets piled high on top of me, and squinting to see in the darkened bedroom, when my father came in to check on his little daughter who was ill with the measles. "How do you feel Giovanna?"

I could barely see him in the dark. "I think I know what a bat must feel like in his hot cave," I answered. "Must I have all these covers Papa?"

He lifted one of the blankets up, but instead of taking it off, he pulled it higher around my neck. "You must stay warm so that you will get better. The baby is coming soon, maybe even today you know."

"But Papa," I began to argue.

"No arguing Giovanna," he replied as he placed his finger on my lips. "Shhh, now tell me, would you like a brother or a sister?"

I don't think I hesitated with my answer. "I definitely want a brother!"

"But why," he asked.

"If it's a girl, Papa," I explained, "she might be prettier than me, and you will love her more!"

Papa looked at me. I could barely see his face with only the tiny stream of light peeking in between the panels of the drapes, but I could tell he was smiling. "No,no Giovanna," he assured me, "I will love you with all my heart forever."

I knew I would accept and love whatever Mama would bring into the world, but deep in my heart, I really didn't want to share my father with anyone else.

6

The new baby was healthy, although his mother was not. After the symptoms became too apparent to ignore, my mother sought medical attention and was diagnosed with tuberculosis (TB). Many of her relatives had already died of the dreaded disease, but my father assured me she had the type of TB that wasn't contagious, and she would only go to the hospital during a TB crisis. (I think my father was just trying to protect me from the possibility of losing my mother.)

As a young girl, the changes that were taking place in our lives were of no consequence to me. I still lacked for nothing, at least nothing that I knew. I had my parents, my brothers, and an army of Jewish relatives. That was all to change.

It was a spectacular sunny day in Tripoli. A warm breeze flowed through our open windows as we enjoyed our noon meal. My mother still paid careful attention to our dinner table—using our beautiful dishes and silverware was a must at every meal. We still owned many pieces of the fine linens that my father once sold. There was never a meal without a beautiful linen tablecloth and napkins at our fingertips.

My mother made special trips to the market for fresh flowers. She loved the color and the aroma that fresh flowers brought to the table. It was one indulgence she refused to eliminate from her life.

As we talked and laughed and listened to the music Papa played for us on the gramophone, there came a knock on our door. It was a family friend, an attorney by the name of Antonio Borrelli. I can still see him standing next to Papa, "What a handsome family you have," he said as he looked around the table at the wife and children of his dear friend. "You are a lucky man *Don Ciccio*," he added as my father invited him to dine with us. He took a chair, and my father immediately poured his friend a glass of wine while my mother brought another plate from the kitchen. When my mother returned to the table with our guest's food, she turned quietly to address Enrico who had laid his head on the table. *"Ricco,"* she said. *"Ricco, alza la testa!"* ("Lift up your head!")

I feared that Enrico would soon feel the wrath of God for being so rude. But he did not answer my mother. She quickly rose and went to him. As she lifted his limp head off of the table, she gasped, "He's burning up with fever!"

Some Italians have a belief in *"Malocchio"* (the Bad Eye). Maybe it was Mr. Borrelli's compliment to our family, maybe not; these things are not for us to know. Enrico fought for eight days with high fevers. The brilliant six-year-old boy, who could already read the paper and converse about worldly affairs, died of spinal meningitis. It was the first and only time I saw my father cry.

A few months after the death of my brother, my mother's health began to deteriorate. She was taken to the hospital where she remained. Still grieving for his lost son and now the possibility of losing his wife, my father was forced to leave the care of his two small children to our housekeeper while he worked.

Through it all, he never stopped taking me to school or picking me up at the end of my classes, although we now walked the distance. Even the horse-drawn carriages that we so often had rode on family outings were a luxury.

It was my favorite time with Papa. I had him all to myself. We talked and laughed, and he listened to my questions and concerns without burdening me with his troubled life. My mind was always thinking of things to ask my father. "Papa," I would ask, "have you ever seen a locust plague?"

"Why do you ask *Piccola*?" Sometimes he liked to answer a question with a question just to tease me.

"Papa!" I would say with my hands on my tiny hips, "have you seen them? Is it true that they are delicious?"

Papa would laugh at my seriousness, "Yes, my silly daughter, I have seen them swoop down from the sky in numbers so great that their swarm would block the sun. I have seen them eat every green plant and not even leave a single blade of grass. But I have never acquired a taste for them." Then he would add for effect, "They are much too crunchy for me."

I would stare at him, trying to determine whether to believe him or not. Had he actually tasted the bug to determine that it was too crunchy? I studied my father's face closely, looking for that devilish grin that was the sure sign that he was teasing me.

7

If I could pick just one day from my young my life that I could change, it would be November 25, 1939. I had expected my father to pick me up from school with his usual gift of roasted chestnuts that he would buy on his way to the school. It was getting late. Unfortunately, I was in the school rotation when my classes were held in the afternoon to early evening. Darkness would soon be upon me. I waited for what seemed an eternity.

Thoughts of walking home entered my mind, but I dared not do such a foolish thing. I thought of the time, not long before Enrico's death, when my brother and I decided to walk through a field of poppies near our home. The flowers were so red and beautiful, so very inviting to touch and pick. Then, out of nowhere, his white robe flapping in the wind like a white-winged bird of prey, the Arab came running straight for us. There was no mistaking his intent; I could feel the hairs on my arms stand at attention. I grabbed my brother's hand, and we ran with all our might until we reached my father's store. Once inside, we both fell to the floor panting like dogs. When we explained to our father what had happened, he became enraged. "Why? Why would you do such a foolish thing? Don't you know how many kidnappings have happened all over the city?" He embraced us, and I could feel his body shaking. "Never, never do such a thing again!"

As those memories flooded my mind, I was also aware of being left at the school alone and with nightfall approaching. The sun's rays began to disappear behind the buildings, leaving the bleached white structures in silhouette. There was nothing else for me to do. I walked home alone for the first time, watching and looking for any suspicious figures who might be lurking in the shadows. The only sounds were the clicking of my shoes on the streets, and my heart beating in my ears.

I knocked and pounded on the door (though I doubt anyone could have heard the efforts of my small hands on the huge wooden door.) No one answered, but my screams finally brought the neighbors out. They helped me push open the door. I went in alone, past my father's stuffed deer and up the stairs. I kept calling, "Papa, Papa!" Guido, who was only two-years-old, was running around the house unsupervised. The housekeeper had undoubtedly gone home at her usual time of four o'clock and had left Guido in the care of my father. After checking all the other rooms, I went to my parents' bedroom. The door to the darkened bedroom was open. I tried to turn on the light, but the switch at the door was not working. I made my way towards the bedside to find the chain to the lamp. I stumbled over something on the floor. Immediately I thought that our housekeeper, Smeranda, had left the rug rolled up by the bed after she had taken it to the balcony to beat the dust from it. I felt my way around the bed until I found the lamp. I was not prepared, not then and not even now as I think of it. In the light, I saw my father lying on the floor; his newspaper was still spread open on the bed. I thought he was just sick, and I bent down and shook him several times. I screamed, "Wake up Papa!" His glasses were broken, and one of his legs was bent under him. The picture in my mind is still so clear. The neighbors, who had followed me up the stairs, pulled me away from my father. I was still screaming for him to wake up and demanding that they let me go to him!

Guido and I were taken to the home of my favorite aunt. My mother, Enrico, Guido, and I had spent many happy days visiting with Aunt Misa, who was actually my mother's aunt. There, we played with cousins and often with the Arab children who lived next door. There were always plenty of delicious Jewish and Arabic dishes to enjoy, stories to share with young and old, and a sense of belonging and joy.

Now, among many of those same relatives, I felt alone and lost. They had gathered to comfort the children of Camilla. They spoke in Hebrew; thinking I couldn't understand, they spoke of my dead father. "The poor child thinks her father is sick. How shall we tell her? How shall we tell Camilla after all she has been through? How shall we tell her that her husband is dead?" I glared at them in disbelief, and I screamed at them that they were wrong! My father was just sick! He would be all right! He was not dead! I knew my Papa would never leave me. I was wrong.

The wake was in our home, as was the tradition. My mother, although weak from the disease that was threatening her own life, discharged herself from the hospital and was home when they laid my father on the bed in the bedroom they had shared so seldom since her illness. To me, Papa looked as if he were sleeping. He wore his favorite suit and vest, and his hands were folded across the top of his belly. He looked no different than when he fell asleep in his blue velvet chair. I had the urge to sit on the bed next to him to search the pockets of his vest for my surprise, and to make sure his gold watch which hung from a chain was still in his lower right vest pocket—but I didn't.

I sat in a chair by the bed and stared at his chest—willing him to breathe. To me, none of what was happening was real. I wanted it to be a bad dream, one that

I would awake from and talk to my father about. I don't remember much else about that day.

PART II
Italy WWII

8

There was unrest in Europe and rumors of the war coming to Libya. My relatives explained to me that Mussolini thought the war would be centered in North Africa, and the Italian colony would be in danger. To insure the safety of the Italian children, Mussolini wanted us to be sent to Italy on holiday for four months, the length of time he thought the war would last. Children ten years and older, supervised by civilians, were the first to leave for Italy.

I thought about the brief explanation that I was given and how much more conversation my father and I would have had, but I knew it was useless for me to ask any more questions about this matter. I was to accept what I was told. To my relatives I was just a ten-year-old child—best seen and not heard.

My mother could not bear the thought of her children in the hands of civilian strangers. She went to the Bishop of the Catholic Church to beg him to help her. My father had been Catholic and very generous to the Church even after his bankruptcy. Camilla might even have promised to become Catholic if only the Church would allow her children to go to Italy under the supervision of the Catholic nuns. My mother knew she would have to return to the hospital, and she wanted desperately to see to the safety of her two remaining children. Although Guido and I were considered Jewish by most people, we were given permission to leave Tripoli with the Franciscan nuns.

Seven months after the death of my father, my half-brother Renzo, then twenty-six-years-old, delivered me to the nuns at the convent in Tripoli. I remember Renzo crying, but I can't remember my reaction to this life-changing event. Although I was leaving my home, my mother, my baby brother, and all that I called my life, the feelings of that day are gone. Perhaps after my father's death, I ceased trying to feel anything.

There were other children at the convent looking forward to our "holiday" in Italy. These Catholic children had been at the convent waiting for their turn to sail. I was there only because my mother had begged.

After a few weeks at the convent, it was finally time for our group of children and nuns to leave. We waited on the docks at the port of Tripoli as the long lines of people boarded the ship, the *Caio Duilio*. I remember the sun being so very bright as it reflected off the emerald waters of the Mediterranean Sea. *"Mare Nos-*

trum" (Our Sea), as Mussolini had us believe, was about to separate me from my family. It was June 10, 1940. Most of the children were happy to be on their way to the motherland. The ship was large and very beautiful, and at that time, I don't remember having any idea that she had been a battleship that had served during World War I, or that she was the sister ship to the *Andrea Doria*, the Italian luxury liner that collided with the Stockholm near Nantucket, Massachusetts many years later.

We were all treated as well as any paying passenger would have been, although as far as I knew, we were traveling at the expense of the Italian government. Our meals were served on beautifully set tables in the ship's dining room. Waiters brought us our meals, and to me, the splendor was a reminder of how it had been before my father lost his fortune. I was saddened by the memory of the time we sailed to Italy as a family on a ship not unlike this one. My thoughts were abruptly interrupted as I became totally engrossed by the dish of delicately carved curls of butter that our waiter had placed before me. I pondered on the process that went into making such a delicate shell design in the butter I was about to spread on my bread.

Two days later, or so it seemed, we arrived in Naples. Thirty-five or forty children from the convent in Tripoli, all girls ages ten to fourteen, left the ship with two nuns, *Suor* (Sister) Renata and *Madre* (Mother) Cristina. *Madre* Cristina was older (who knows how old—my perception of age was so different at ten) and came from a very aristocratic family. She was as strict as she was proper, and we dared not misbehave in front of her. We all feared the flesh-twisting pinch she would administer on our bare young arms if we dared to cross her.

Suor Renata was young, perhaps in her twenties. Her eyes were bright blue like the sky on a spring morning, and from the moment I met her, I had a burning curiosity about the color of her hair that she wore hidden under her head covering. All the girls loved the youthful spirit of Sister Renata, her love for life, for us, and especially for her God. I sensed her love and compassion and I felt protected. She was not only our teacher and confidant, but also our friend.

From the Port of Naples we traveled by train to the Italian town of Cattolica on the Adriatic Sea. We were astounded by the beautiful scenery we witnessed from the train. Olive trees and grapevines were budding with the promise of a bountiful fall crop. Green hills and farms, flowers of every color—it was a wonderful site and so different from the North African city we had left.

The fancy beach resort at Cattolica was host to many Italian families and foreigners who went there to enjoy their summer holidays. We were there on our holiday as well. Our days were spent playing on the sand and swimming in the sea. We had no idea about the war as we awaited the end of summer to return to Tripoli, our families, and school.

At the end of the summer season the resort closed, and we now discovered we could not return to Tripoli. The fighting in North Africa had escalated. Ships were being sunk in the Mediterranean Sea—our crossing to home was no longer safe!

9

Again we boarded the train, this time back to Naples. I was reunited with my brother Guido who had sailed on the next voyage of the *Caio Duilio* after me. He had remained in Naples for the summer. Guido was just three-years-old and had traveled from Tripoli with another group of nuns and younger children. His voyage on the *Caio Duilio* was to be the last trip the ship would make before it was sunk by the British as it was anchored in the port of Taranto, Italy in November of 1940. The war had come to Italy!

All the children who had been brought to Italy from Tripoli with the order of the *Francescane Missionarie di Maria*, were now reunited in a convent on the outskirts of Naples that had once been an ancient feudal castle. (I have no idea what became of the children who were entrusted to the civilians.)

The castle stood on the top of a hill in Arenella, a small town overlooking Naples. Beautiful lush flower gardens, along with olive and fruit trees adorned the grounds around the castle. In the distance, especially at night, I could see the volcanic glow of the never-sleeping Mount Vesuvius. Huge iron gates gave entrance through gray stone walls and the remnants of the mote that once had protected the fortress.

It felt so strange to be there, but at the same time, the whole idea of being in an ancient castle was exciting. My young mind often pictured what it must have been like hundreds and hundreds of years before. I wondered about the people that had lived in the castle and often imagined a Prince riding through the iron gates on his Arabian stallion—coming, of course, to claim the hand of Princess Giovanna. My silly thoughts were a way of occupying my mind and my restless heart that longed to be home with my family. My only consolation was that I was with my brother Guido. Although the girls and boys were kept in separate quarters, I was able to see him whenever I wanted. He was my link to home.

The castle was enormous with thick stone walls and cold stone floors. It was not only void of color, but bare of furnishings as well. The nuns used only the bare essentials: tables, chairs, and beds. Although they were very uncomfortable, our beds where the only things that mattered to us at the end of a long exhausting day. The nuns worked very hard to make life as normal as possible for the children, but they had very strict rules. Every morning without fail the nuns would get us out of bed before sunrise—one way or the other. It was, after all, a convent.

Throughout our sleeping quarters the groans and moans from the sleepy girls fell on deaf ears. *"Svegliatevi bambine. É l'ora di andare a Messa. Fate un fioretto per la pace."* ("Wake up little girls. It's time to go to Mass. Make an offering for peace.") *"Non voglio andare—voglio dormire."* ("I don't want to go—I want to sleep.") I groaned. Regardless of my complaining, I was always one of the first girls dressed. For that reason, the nuns paid little attention to me—they just let me gripe and moan. I truly hated getting out of bed, after all, Guido and I weren't really Catholic. I playfully thought we should just be treated like guests. My opinions were of little value—we were all on our knees before the sun had barely made it into the sky.

Sometimes I would see my brother's tiny head barely peeking over the top of the pew, and I would try to get his attention. "Guido," I whispered.

Guido would turn and smile at me with mischief in his eyes. Knowing how easily Guido could become rambunctious and not wanting him to get into trouble, I waved and motioned for him to turn back around.

"Me?" He mouthed as he pointed his finger to his chest.

"Si," I whispered as I again motioned for him to turn.

Sister Renata looked over at us and cleared her throat—twice! Guido immediately turned around, and I put my head down in prayerful submission.

Naples

10

Somehow the nuns discovered that German soldiers were actively seeking Jewish families being hidden by the Italians. I believe the nuns thought Guido and I might be in danger. To help protect us, I was asked if Guido and I would like to be baptized into the Catholic religion. I respected the nuns of the convent, especially Sister Renata. My father had been Catholic, and I knew he would be pleased. I said yes. In January of 1941, I was baptized and confirmed on the same day—a very unusual practice. Usually these ceremonies are done years apart. My new baptismal name became Giovanna Vittoria Iris Fiorenza Maria Bonifazio. Guido received his sacraments a week later.

My godmother was a professor of literature at the university and was related to the Mother Superior at the convent. To honor my godmother, I took part of her name, Fiorenza, as part of my baptismal name. Fiorenza D'Amelio had taken a liking to me soon after I arrived at the convent. She thought I was intelligent and showed much promise. My *madrina* (godmother) was born of Italian nobility. She was older (again I can't say how old) than most of the nuns in the convent and had never been married. She was to become my mentor and a very important part of my life.

I was a good girl and very studious. Reading was one of my favorite pass times. It allowed me to travel to far away places and meet many wonderful and exotic people. It was also an escape from the reality of my life.

Learning came easy to me—everything, that is, except mathematics. My mind formed a block when it came to mathematical figures. I had an exceptional aptitude for languages. I had already learned a great deal of Arabic, Hebrew, Latin, and of course, my native language of Italian. Now I was learning French by listening to the nuns.

There were times when I threw caution and brains out the window, and my fearlessness would get the better of me. Sister Renata's hair was always covered, as were the heads of all the nuns. I used to fantasize about what she might look like in regular street clothes, and I was particularly curious about the color of her hair. She had blue eyes and very light colored eyebrows. I suspected she was probably a blond, but then again, she could have had red or light brown hair. My curiosity was killing me! I was determined to see her hair.

One night I waited until I was certain all the other girls were asleep. Slowly I crept out of my bed and tiptoed across the room. I hid behind the curtain that surrounded Sister Renata's bed and waited. Soon she came to her bedside. My anticipation was excruciating. I covered my mouth with my hand to keep the giggle I felt in my stomach from bursting forth. Her practiced hands moved quickly, removing the hair pins that held her head covering in place. In an instant, she had removed it. Finally, there it was—the blondest head of hair I had ever seen. In my excitement, I stood up from my hiding place and yelled out so all could hear, *"Ahhh è bionda!"* ("She's blonde!") I'll never know how I didn't cause Sister Renata to have a heart attack!

Although I expected her reaction and my punishment to be horrendous, Sister Renata seemed to have a difficult time refraining from laughter. She did her best to act as if she were upset with me, but I could see the hint of a grin on her face. After a short scolding, she sent me to my bed to say a Rosary and an Act of Contrition. That night I lay in my bed with a huge smile on my face. Sister Renata was every bit as beautiful on the outside as she was on the inside.

I really tried to conduct myself like the well-mannered young girl the nuns bragged about, but sometimes it was very difficult. A part of me wanted to run and play and eat my fill of the fruit that hung so invitingly on the trees surrounding the castle. I wanted to talk and visit with my friends and my brother whenever I felt like it. Just once I would have liked to tell the nuns I didn't feel like getting up early for church that day. I was staying in bed! And they would listen to me.

When the message was given to me to report to Mother Superior immediately, I was truly stressed. I pondered and pondered over what she could possibly discipline me about; a summons from Mother Superior was never good news. I had no idea what I had done. I quietly entered her little office. "You wanted to see me Mother Superior?"

"Giovanna," she began, "sit down child. Is there something troubling you, something you need to talk about?" I slowly shook my head from side to side as I tried to recollect the misdeeds of the past few days. I truly didn't know my sin. She continued, "Maybe you would like to talk with Father Joseph. Giovanna, I am concerned about you."

"But Mother Superior," I answered, "I don't know what I need to talk to anyone about. What have I done?" It occurred to me that perhaps my thoughts had somehow found their way to the surface. They weren't evil thoughts, just a little mischievous perhaps, certainly nothing to warrant a meeting with Mother Superior, and worse yet, Father Joseph!

Finally, she shook her head, "Alright Giovanna, perhaps I shall have to help you remember. It has come to my attention that you have not been receiving Holy Communion with the others during Mass. It is because you need to confess some sin first?"

My relief must have shown immediately as I jumped up from my seat and let out a huge sigh. I could see the startled look on Mother Superior's face at my abrupt actions. "I was just hungry!" I stated matter-of-factly. The fast which was required of us from midnight until Communion was too much for me; I had been sneaking out early in the mornings to the gardens and climbing into the branches of the tangerine tree. My sin was the juicy Neapolitan tangerines.

11

The other girls used to call me "*La Principessa dei Piselli*" ("The Princess of the Peas") after the fable about a young girl who was identified as the true princess when she was unable to sleep on her bed because she could feel a pea under her mattress. I didn't try to be different, but the nuns said I was delicate and wouldn't subject me to hard or strenuous work. They used me as an example when they wanted the other girls to observe and learn table manners. They would say, "Look at Giovanna and learn." That was more than enough reason to cause the other girls to make fun of me. I sometimes resented being "the proper one"; I would have liked to appear tougher. But the memory of that time is not a bad one, the teasing was all in fun, and there was never any bad treatment towards each other or from the nuns.

Most of our days were spent in class with the nuns and a few civilian teachers. If we weren't studying or praying, we would help with chores. The nuns kept us busy—after all, we were no longer on holiday.

During our recreation time, we played games or walked in the beautiful lush gardens or listened to the nuns as they read the classics to us. My favorite story was "The Count of Monte Cristo." I looked forward to the few pages the nuns would read to us each night. That was before the bombing began.

The first planes came in the daytime, and we strained our eyes against the brightness of the sun to watch them. The nuns said the planes were taking photographs, although I wondered how they knew. All the children would watch in awe as the silver birds roared across the sky. The sheer force of the sound made my insides quiver.

The first time the air raids began we were all in bed. I could hear the bombs exploding in the distance. It was the most thunderous noise I had ever heard. It was not long before I could distinguish between the bombs that were exploding at a distance, and the ones that were very close to us. Each one fell from the sky with a scream—eeeeeeeeeeee! The accuracy of the bombs was questionable at best, and the convent was in as much danger as any military target. Sirens from Naples and neighboring towns could be heard wailing their eerie warnings of an approaching air raid. Sometimes the sirens, which were supposed to be the fore-warning of the air raids, came after the bombings began. Naples fell in darkness every night. No one was allowed to even burn a candle where the glow might be seen from the air.

The nuns had already prepared. Each night that the sirens wailed, we got out of our beds in an orderly fashion and followed the nuns to the lower levels of the castle. Only the nuns were allowed to talk as they gave us instructions. We gathered in a large room directly under the castle. In that dark and dank space there were blankets, chairs, candles and meager amounts of food and water. There was a mixture of fear and excitement in the children. We were instructed to sit quietly while a count would be taken of all the children. We huddled together—girls, boys, and nuns. Soft whimpering from some of the children caused uneasiness among the rest of us. We realized this was not a game, but we had no idea what was happening outside the walls of our fortress.

When all the children were accounted for, we would pray the Rosary while the sirens screamed one after another. The soft chanting of our prayers grew louder and more urgent with each bomb that fell.

This exhausting routine became an almost nightly event. Before retiring for the night we would look up at the night sky, if the stars were out, we knew the planes would come! Many of us lay in our beds unable to sleep. Oh how I needed my father to explain all of this to me. I refused to cry as I waited in dreaded anticipation for the next bomb to fall. My only protection was the bedcovers over my head. When the bombs were really close, the nuns took us even farther down underground into the bowels of the castle. Perhaps some of these rooms were parts of the castle's dungeon once, I wasn't sure. Could we have inherited the same horrible fate that awaited the enemy of ancient royalty as they waited their doom beneath the floors of the castle? It seemed that way to me. I hated it! These cave-like rooms and passages were built during the Feudal times when castles fought each other. Those who needed to escape had dug tunnels under the gardens and down the hill. The well-hidden exit to the underground escape routes gave those ancient castle dwellers a chance for survival from invading armies.

Children and nuns scurried down the path of what seemed to be the walls of a vertical cave. Down, down, down we went following the nuns' lanterns. The dismal light created eerie shadows on the walls of the passages as we scurried down into the earth. All the children formed one continuous line as we held on to each other. The dampness and the cold chilled my bones, and there, I think, for the first time, I was truly afraid.

It was so far down, so deep and dark, that I would have gladly stayed and taken my chances above ground. I knew the exit to our underground passage was now blocked, and I feared being trapped and buried alive. With tons and tons of earth over the top of us, we could hear nothing—not the sirens, not the planes, not the explosions—not any sounds of life beyond our muffled cries.

Little did I know that many citizens of Naples were also escaping underground. There were many places under the city to hide, from the ancient Roman aqueducts to the underground caverns and old quarries. All of Naples and the surrounding areas had been forced into hiding like scared moles!

There came a point when we all became so tired of the nightly ritual, that all we wanted was to sleep in our beds all night. At times when we went below and the count was taken, someone would be missing; someone had decided they would rather die in bed. The nuns would ask for a volunteer to return upstairs during an air raid to find the missing girl or boy. I always wanted to be picked to go—mainly to be above ground, but also because I always thought I was braver and smarter than the rest of the girls even though I was small (and according to the nuns delicate) for my age. It never occurred to me that my thoughts of superiority were a form of vanity.

One particular time, I went upstairs to find my classmate and found her not asleep, but jumping from one bed to another as if to dare a bomb to hit her. I could not blame my classmate, but it was my duty to save her. Many of us would have rather died in our beds after a time. I sat the lantern down and was forced to go in hot pursuit! I jumped from bed to bed until I caught her by the pigtails (which we all wore back then) and dragged her by the hair down the stairs. The other girls cheered and clapped while the nuns thanked God.

12

The air raids continued for months, and I wondered what more could be destroyed. We had no news from home nor were any Italians allowed to listen to a radio to know what was happening with the war. We were not to be influenced by the propaganda that was being aired through the radio waves. If caught with a radio, one was certain to be jailed or hung.

The nuns refused to let our spirits die. They did all in their power to be mother and father to us. Often the children would huddle together and sing of home and country. *"Mamma...e per la vita non ti lascio mai più...."* ("Mama...and for life I will never leave you again....") It's all we had; it was our song of home. As we sang, our minds drifted to better times, happier times, and we all cried together.

Our food supplies were now scarce. Much of Naples and neighboring towns lay in ruin, as did the fields and vineyards. In spite of this, the nuns saw to it that we did not go hungry. They went into town several times a week to plead with the farmers for any scraps of food they could spare for the children. Sometimes all they could find were apples, and that is all we ate for a while. I would have rather eaten the cooked apples than the powdered green peas—they were awful and made me throw up.

As the children outgrew their clothing, the nuns sewed them new garments from blankets or any piece of material they could find. They gathered old shoes and somehow made us new ones from the old leather. Although I have no idea how, they made soap for us as well. The Franciscan nuns were missionaries whose purpose in life was to serve and help the people of God. It was unfortunate their convents were not intended to house visitors, and especially not equipped for the nurturing of children. Even so, in my mind, they performed small miracles each and every day. They never complained. They would take the food from their own mouths, rather than to see any of us go hungry. They were truly angels in the depths of hell.

The bombing was relentless. Naples was in shambles and eventually our food supply was nearly non-existent. One day the nuns gathered all the children together in the chapel.

"Children," Mother Superior began as a hush fell over the room, "in a few days we will be sending the girls to the convent in Rovereto." Surprised exchanges could be heard among the children.

"Quiet!" One of the nuns commanded.

"As I was saying, only the girls will be going. Unfortunately there is only room for the girls."

"Why?" asked a frightened voice from among the children.

Someone else asked, "Where is Rovereto?"

"Quiet!"

"I know all of you have questions, and I will try to answer them the best I can. We have very little food or supplies here for all of you. The convent in Rovereto has only room enough for half of you. We have decided to send the girls. The boys and the rest of us will remain here. We will make do. God is with us."

"Northern Italy—how could I go so far away from Guido," I thought. I immediately looked over at my baby brother. I don't think he was old enough to understand all that was happening, but by the way he was looking at me, I could tell he knew things were about to change for him again. His big brown eyes seemed to stare past me, and then he just looked down at the ground as streams of tears rolled down his cheeks. I made my way to him and held him tightly. There was nothing short of running away that we could do. But that, of course, was sure suicide and I would never have put him in more danger. I was forced to acknowledge my helplessness. The air raids in Naples had not stopped; I knew I might never see Guido again.

There seemed to be no time to spare. The girls and a few nuns gathered meager belongings and prepared to travel to the upper most region of Italy bordering Austria. We traveled by foot for most of the day until we reached a town north of Naples with a train station. Reluctantly, I boarded the train that would separate me from my baby brother. The train was full of people trying to escape Naples and the surrounding areas. Packed into the train like a can of sardines, we were forced to stand for the long journey to Northern Italy.

Castle di Rovereto was the home of another order of the Franciscan and in the most beautiful mountain setting I had ever seen. The small town in the Trentino Region of Italy was nestled due south of the Brenner Pass in the Alps. Rows and rows of vineyards draped the side of hills and mountainsides. Crystal clear lakes and streams dotted the hills and valleys. It must have been in the fall of 1942 when we arrived at the convent. Grapes were being harvested throughout the region. Sweet clusters of fruit filled the baskets of the harvesters. After a diet of cooked apples, powdered green peas, and scraps of bread, grapes were a wonderful treat. The war had not reached this place. It was so peaceful and serene in comparison to the hell we had escaped in Naples. I filled my lungs with fresh, clean mountain air—trying to replace and purge the memory of the stale air beneath the castle and the scent of death and destruction in Naples. It was as though I had never breathed before that very moment. My thoughts drifted to my brother, "Oh how wonderful this place would be for Guido." Tears streamed down my cheeks as I thought of him and the danger he was in.

To support the convent, the nuns raised silkworms in the basement and sold the silk thread. There were trays and trays of fat, hungry worms. The children were allowed to help pick the leaves of the mulberry bush to feed the worms and, of course, pick berries for ourselves. Once I ate so many berries, I was sick for the rest of the day.

Rovereto

As a young girl born in the arid heat of the deserts of North Africa, I found the icy cold winter in Rovereto to be a different kind of hell than the bombing I had experienced in Naples. Winters started early in this place in the pre-Alps. Each day we walked to school from the convent with little regard for the weather. Snow and ice covered the fields, roads, and mountains. My hands were so cold that I could barely bend my fingers to hold my books. Our garments only served as minimal protection against the elements. There was no heat from any source in our classrooms or in the convent. I remember having to force my pen into my frozen fist when I arrived to my class. (I still have a scar on my hand from the frostbite.)

At night, the bed I would have died to stay in when in Naples, was now a sheet of ice to my young skin. Even with my body in the fetal position under the worn-thin blanket, and my hands tucked under my armpits, I shivered until exhaustion finally gave way to sleep. Here too the nuns would nudge us out of bed in the mornings, but unlike in Naples where I was nearly always one of the first to be ready for Mass, in this icy atmosphere, my body refused to respond. If crying would have helped, I am sure I would have cried an ocean, but the water would have surely frozen on my face. My frigid body moved in slow motion. Every breath I took produced a tiny white cloud that streamed from between chattering teeth. My trembling fingers labored to put on my garments for Mass and school. Although I loved soap and water and cleanliness, I would not dare plunge my hands into the icy mountain water. Two fingers barely moistened and rubbed into the corners of my eyes was the best I could do in the mornings. I swore that never in my life was I going to be that cold again.

My time in Rovereto was to be short. After enduring most of the winter, three other girls and I were chosen by the nuns to be sent to a convent in Florence to further our education and attend the university. We were the most promising students, possibly the future educators or doctors—who knew! The nuns never ceased to have our best interest at heart and were determined to give us our chance at a better life. With the sorrow of leaving my friends, again we said our good-byes and began the journey that would change our lives.

It was not until years later that I learned that Rovereto, the one place the nuns had thought would be safe for the children, had, in fact, sustained heavy damage from the bombing that occurred shortly after I left. The convent had been completely destroyed. I have no idea what became of the remaining children that had been left there. It was my destiny to have been sent away.

13

Agnese was the oldest of the four girls traveling to Florence. Her family had originally come from Northern Italy. Her thick red hair was the perfect compliment to her blue eyes and fair complexion. She was tall and strong in body and mind. Her looks were inherent of Northern European ancestry. Agnese also spoke German—an invaluable blessing to us in the coming months. There would be times when I would come to rely and depend on Agnese as if she were my own mother.

Stefanina was a stunning beauty. She was half Italian and half Arabic, and wore a henna tattoo on her forehead. Her long wavy hair was as black as the night and accentuated her dark eyes and caramel colored skin. Her beauty was enhanced by her slim, tall figure, which I envied more than I cared to admit. Stefanina was a very devout Catholic and found strength and peace in her meditations and prayers.

The third girl was Carmela. She was most like me in height, complexion, and ancestry. Her family was from Sicily, as was my father's. Her olive skin and dark eyes were common in the southern parts of Italy. For some reason, Carmela left less of an impression on my mind; I remember very little of her.

I was the youngest of the four girls and regretfully, the smallest. I had always hoped to be tall like my mother, but I was almost fourteen and had not yet reached five feet. I was told that I was beautiful during the rare times the other girls at the convents and I indulged in conversation about such things as looks, or boys, or other silly talk. Many thought I resembled a little Italian doll. I knew my friends meant well, but being called a doll was just a reminder of my small stature. They said I had almond shaped eyes, although I never looked at myself long enough to know their shape. My eyes were dark brown like my mother's, and my eyesight was poor like my father—that much I did know.

Living with the nuns taught us to see our bodies as holy temples. Looking at ourselves in the mirror for more than a few seconds was interpreted as vanity. Although I seldom looked in a mirror (and if I did, it was a quick glance at best), my thick auburn braids were always parted equally. I would comb and brush my waist-length hair, then braid it all by feel. Even dressing and undressing were done so that no one could see our naked bodies. I became quite adept at dressing myself completely for daytime with my nightclothes still on. Then at night, I would put my nightgown on before I removed my street clothes. It was an art form.

The nuns taught us to be modest and private about our bodies. There were never conversations about bodily functions—not the normal ones that everyone had, or the ones that only a female must live through. I had questions, many questions about the changes that were taking place in my body, but fear and embarrassment kept me from asking anyone. My body was developing rapidly and with it came strange belly cramping and breast tenderness.

As the train weaved through the mountains and valleys on its way to Florence, I thought about the time two years before in Naples. There had been a particular room in the convent in the old castle where only the older or a select few of the girls were allowed to enter. No one would tell me what took place in that secret room, and of course, my curiosity was torturous.

One day I approached my friend Anna as she was leaving the secret room. *"Ciao Anna,"* I said as I pretended to bump into her.

"Ciao Giovanna," she replied. "What are you doing here?"

"Oh," I said innocently, "I was looking for Sister Renata. Have you seen her?"

"I think she is in there Giovanna, helping Carmela." She pointed to the room.

"Va bene (alright)*,* I will go in there and get her."

"No Giovanna, you cannot!"

"But why? Can't you tell me?"

Anna looked around. For a moment I thought she had fallen for my charade.

"No, Giovanna! It is not my place to tell you. You will find out soon enough!"

My face must have shown my disappointment. Not even my friend would tell me about the room!

Finally, when I was twelve-years-old—after months of cramping, swelling, and soreness, I learned the truth about the room the hard way. Fearing that what was happening to me was some punishment from God, or perhaps that I might be dying, I finally went to Sister Renata.

"What is happening to me?" I cried as I showed her my soiled garments. "Am I being punished by God? Am I dying?"

Sister Renata smiled as she held me in her arms. "Shhh, Giovanna, you are not dying, and what could God possibly punish you for my little angel?" After assuring me that death was not upon me, she took me by the hand, and we entered the secret room together.

As I discovered, only the girls suffering with their "monthly visitor" could use this room to take care of their needs. Embarrassment was probably one of the biggest factors in keeping the room a secret. Although we would all become accustomed to this "monthly visitor", the nuns could not give us a thorough explanation of why this was happening at all. "You are becoming a woman," is the best way they could explain this strange affliction.

Once in the secret room, Renata set up a basin of water for me and showed me what I needed to do. None of the girls ever had to wash a single soiled garment. The nuns took care of everything for us. We just need not talk about any of it!

I smiled as I thought of that time nearly two years before at the convent in Arenella—that seemed so long ago. My thoughts jumped back into the present time as the four of us, Agnese, Stefanina, Carmela and I, accompanied by two nuns rode the train to Florence. A strong bond had formed between us almost immediately. We were young, intelligent women with the hope of bright futures ahead of us. We thanked God for our good fortune. We knew we had been given an opportunity to live and to learn that the other children from Tripoli might never be able to enjoy. We also knew we might be alone in the world, that we might never see our families in Tripoli again, or our brothers and sisters left behind in Naples.

14

Florence was more beautiful than I had imagined. My love for the arts, history, and music had finally found the heart of the Italian Renaissance. It was already apparent as we crossed into western Italy that this region known as *Toscana* (Tuscany) was one of the most breathtaking places we had ever seen. Tall slender cypress trees marched in line across rolling hills. Farms and vineyards formed beautiful quilts of colors. Castles and medieval villages dotted hilltops. Everything here seemed in order—peaceful.

Florence

We crossed over the Arno River on the bridge, *Ponte alla Carraia*, to reach the convent in *Piazza del Carmine* where we would live. The convent was surprisingly beautiful as well. As I entered through the huge wooden doors to the convent, I dared to feel some form of happiness that was long overdue.

We were greeted with open arms by this new order of the Franciscan nuns. As our own nuns became acquainted with our new hosts, my three companions and I were taken to our living quarters. The nuns lived in a cloister, a part of the building that was off limits to anyone but themselves. The four of us shared a room across the courtyard in a building behind the main convent. Each of us had a small bed and a tiny space for our meager belongings. My bed was nearest to the window, which suited me just fine. I loved the light from the sun, and abhorred darkness in any form. I don't remember feeling that way until after my experiences below the castle in Arenella.

Each morning we attended Mass at *Santa Maria del Carmine* Catholic Church in the same piazza. This second century church had been completely destroyed by fire and rebuilt in the eighteenth century. Between prayers I would gaze at the beautiful frescoes that had been painted centuries before by the artists Masolino, Masaccio, and Lippi, and I marveled at the beautiful stained glass windows that surrounded the walls of the cathedral. After Mass, my friends and I parted ways; each of us going to a different school for our age group and school major.

With my books in my arms, I walked down the streets of the city greeting the shopkeepers as I passed. *"Buongiorno"* ("Good morning"), I would say.

"Buongiorno signorina," they would answer.

The streets of Florence were rather quiet in comparison to the streets of Naples at this hour. In Naples one could smell the wonderful odors of freshly baked bread and pastries permeating the morning air. All up and down the streets of Naples, through their open windows, I could hear music and the loud voices of busy Neapolitan families as they prepared for the new day, and the wonderful aroma of freshly brewed Italian coffee from their kitchens. The sight of clean laundry drying from lines strung between the second stories of two adjacent buildings was a common site in Naples, and it often reminded me of colored banners—it seemed almost festive.

In contrast, the people of Florence were more reserved—at least within the city. There was a sense of pride in their cultural achievements, their history, the music, and the art which was in abundance in this city. Dante, Leonardo Da Vinci, and Michelangelo were just a few of the famous people who had lived, studied, and worked in this marvelous place. Unlike Neapolitans, people in Florence seemed to keep their household business and conversations behind closed windows and doors. Rarely would one see laundry hanging from their buildings.

While walking to school, I often stopped long enough to gaze upon the sunrise over the beautiful city and to admire the magnificent *Ponte Vecchio*, one of the most famous bridges in Italy. Flowers hung from windows and balconies, birds sang, and church bells rang throughout the city. I smiled and often sang as I continued on to school. I was truly in love with Florence!

Through the insistence and guidance of the nuns, I attended not only a school for academic studies, but also a music school run by the *Canossian* nuns. I was never more at home with any of my studies. My vocal training consisted of endless hours of sight-reading and *solfeggio*, a vocal exercise that was very difficult to master. Often I found myself singing the scales through the streets of Florence.

At night we attended the vespers, the evening prayers. In the *piazza* (town square) at sunset, the church bells rang to remind the faithful to come to pray the Rosary. There was something melancholic about the sound of the evening bells. Many times I sat in church listening to the bells and huge tears would flow from my eyes as I thought of my family. The day was done. It had begun in prayer and happiness, and had ended in prayer and tears.

Santa Maria del Carmine Catholic Church
Modern day Florence

There were no air raids in Florence. I was told the city was protected by the Geneva Convention because of its abundance of history and art treasures. For whatever reason, I was thankful. My studies consumed me, as did the city. The Italian people here spoke with such clarity, that their vernacular flowed like music. I learned to speak better Italian than I had at any other time in life. This city, with its endless beauty and culture seemed to complete me.

Giovanna in Florence
1943

15

The presence of German soldiers was a constant reminder that our country was at war. They were everywhere—in the streets, on top of buildings, and always heavily armed. It became common knowledge, although not anything one would talk freely about in public, that the soldiers would steal art and loot the homes of the Italians, and do whatever else they could get away with. Many Italians had their fill of the Germans and the Fascist movement and openly rebelled. To help stop the relentless march of Fascism, the partisans (those opposing Mussolini) often fought brother against brother against the German stronghold.

On one day, not unlike any other, I walked home from class as I normally did. As I neared the *Piazza del Carmine*, I became aware of an unusual amount of activity in the streets. German soldiers were arming machine guns. People in the street began screaming at me, *"Corri bambina!"* ("Run little girl!") I clutched my books in my arms and began running toward the door of the convent. My heart was pounding as I realized that the nuns kept the convent door locked. I had no where else to go. Just as I approached the door, I turned to look at the Germans. They had begun firing the guns at civilians in the street, "tatatata!" My body became limp as I turned around to face my executioners. I leaned against the door. The blood drained from my face, and my voice became a tiny squeak, "No, no, no!"

Just then I felt myself being grabbed from behind. I immediately turned. The nuns, who had been anxiously waiting for me, quickly opened the huge door and dragged me into the safety of the convent. I later learned that a German soldier had been killed the night before, probably by a partisan. Unfortunately, the Germans would kill many innocent people in retaliation for the death of one of their own.

The convent was not impregnable. German soldiers often barged in demanding the nuns turn over any Jews they were hiding. Although the nuns denied such accusations, in truth, there were Jews hidden in the convent, as were the other three young women and I when such raids occurred.

One refugee was an elderly Jewish woman whom the nuns had been protecting. I read to her each evening, and she was delighted over my own Jewish ancestry. I reminded her that I was now a Catholic, and no one must know that my mother was Jewish. She insisted that if my maternal line was Jewish, then I too was Jewish no matter what anyone said. It was God's law! There was no use in arguing with her because I knew she was right. I had repeatedly heard the same explanation from my mother's relatives. But as long as no one turned me over to the Germans, being Catholic and Italian during this time would help to keep me alive.

I continued visiting and reading to my Jewish friend until the night I entered her room and saw her teeth in a glass of water. Never having seen such an atrocity, I screamed and ran back to my room. The other girls could not contain their laughter as I tried to tell them the horrible sight I had seen! During the following days, they never missed a chance to tease me about the old lady's teeth!

There was no laughter on Sunday, November 27, 1943. It was only three o'clock in the morning when the nuns' warning bells caused us to jump out of our beds and hide. Nearly thirty German soldiers and Italian Secret Service forced their way into the convent. The loud voices of the soldiers were frightening as they marched through the convent and adjoining buildings. Almost immediately, two soldiers entered our room and dragged the four of us to the main convent building.

"We know you have Jews here! Turn them over to us now, or we will be forced to find them ourselves!" The German soldier's voice was menacing.

Mother Superior spoke, "I assure you that you are gravely mistaken! We are here alone. You are invading a private sanctuary, and you must leave!"

The soldier aimed his rifle toward the floor and shot! Everyone jumped at the sudden explosion of gunfire. I held my hand over my mouth to suppress my scream. The convent floor was riddled with similar gunshot holes from other times the soldiers had done this very thing. But the other times were meant as warnings against befriending Jews—this time was not.

The nuns tried to block the soldiers' entrance to their cloister. "This is our sleeping quarters! There are only our elderly sisters in their beds in these rooms."

"Move aside!" demanded one of the soldiers as he pushed Mother Superior to the floor. "We are not here to harm you, but we will search these rooms at all costs!"

Mother Superior was frantic. "I beg of you, in the name of God, please do not enter. You will surely cause great pain and stress to our elderly!" The soldier kicked her down once again. The other nuns left their post to help her.

The soldiers searched from room to room looking for hidden Jews, and did not stop until they found what they were looking for. The nuns retreated—they were helpless in stopping the inevitable.

Within a few hours, eighty Jewish women and children were found hidden in the attic of the convent. Soft whimpering and crying filled the convent as the German and Italian soldiers stripped the Jews of their few belongings. For several days the captives were interrogated—some were beaten as they waited for the trucks to arrive that would take them to Auschwitz.

One young girl got away through a bathroom window. I never knew who that girl was—perhaps my mind played tricks on me. To this day I cannot say for certain that I was not that girl. I see that window so clearly in my mind; it was small and high up on the wall. Only a small person could have fit through the tight opening, perhaps someone with the presence of mind to think her ancestry would have had a negative affect on her life during this monstrous invasion. Someone who had friends that may have helped her up to the window—there are no other memories after that one moment, that one vision!

Stairs to the attic of the convent.

16

The pounding on the convent doors was relentless. The angry voices of German soldiers sent everyone scurrying again. As one of the nuns unlocked the door, the soldiers barged in, guns and rifles in hand. They were screaming, *"Nord, nord!"* and pointing toward the river. The other three girls and I huddled together in our room, not knowing what to expect. I was fairly certain there were no other Jews left to find in the convent. I wondered if they had come for me!

There was no time to hide. "What are they saying Agnese?" My voice trembled. "They want us to go north," she replied, "they say the Americans are coming." It was August 1944.

One of the nuns came running to our room. "Quickly, quickly, gather a few things and come with us. We must leave the convent!" Immediately she returned to the main building.

The four of us looked at each other in bewilderment. "Where are we going?" Carmela was the first to ask.

We looked to Agnese, the oldest of us, for direction. "I am not sure," she admitted, "just get a jacket and put on your shoes."

"But Agnese," I began, "what is happening?"

"I don't know Giovanna—just hurry before the soldiers come to get us!"

We quickly gathered a few belongings and joined the nuns in the main building of the convent. There was much commotion outside, and when the doors of the convent were opened we could see herds of people in the streets being pushed towards the river by the German soldiers. We followed the nuns out of the convent. Agnese stopped and looked at the three of us as we stepped out onto the plaza. "Do not let go of my hand, Giovanna. All of us must hold hands. Do you understand?" We all nodded, so thankful for Agnese's rational thinking in all the chaos.

Thousands of people on the south side of the river were now trying to cross the bridges over the Arno River to the north side of Florence. Children were crying as they were being pulled in carts or carried by their parents. Babies wailed from interrupted meals, and some still hung to their mother's breast. Men and women shouted obscenities to one another in their frustration. Barking dogs added to the commotion and confusion! People trying to bring carts with some possessions found it impossible to move in the crowds of panic stricken human flesh. Gunfire and explosions accelerated the fear. People lost all rational thinking and were guided with only the need for self-preservation.

We got to the bridge with the nuns, but soon lost sight of them. Our bodies were swept with the movement of the crowds; we managed to hang on to each other. Our voices were drowned by the masses. Agnese and Stefanina, the two taller girls, made sure that Carmela and I held on to them as we were being pushed and shoved across the bridge. When we finally reached the other side of the river, hundreds of frightened people were making their way through the streets of Florence. No one knew where they were going. We were just going north out of Florence!

The four of us climbed up hills and down into valleys we had never been through before in our life. We walked and walked until our legs gave out. We had no food or water and not a clue of what to do next. We had never been that far north of the city, but we continued walking up and down the hilly countryside until nearly nightfall. The people of Florence had taken a hundred different directions after leaving the city. Luckily for some, there was family in other parts of the region for them to find shelter. But for us, four young women from North Africa, there was no one.

After some time, we spotted what appeared to be another convent at the top of a hill. This, we decided, was our only hope, and we forced ourselves up the hill led only by our thirst, hunger, and the fading rays of the sun.

We pounded and pounded on the door, begging the nuns to let us in! "Help us! Please help us!" We screamed in unison.

"In God's name," begged Stefanina, "help us!"

In our frantic state of mind, we yelled out the name of our convent, of our Mother Superior, and the name of any nun we could think of.

"We only want shelter from the night, food, and water—please," Agnese pleaded. "Please let us in!"

Finally, an eternity later, the door opened, and four tearful, hysterical young women fell to the floor at the feet of their benefactors. We knew the nuns were being very cautious; many people were seeking safety that night. They quickly showed us to a room and told us to be very quiet. After a few bites of bread and cheese, and a drink of water, four very exhausted young women lay side by side on a blanket on the floor and quickly fell asleep.

When we arose the next morning, the nuns told us it was a miracle we had made it up the hill the night before. In every window of the convent, German soldiers stood guard and would shoot anyone attempting to infiltrate their fortress. Through the grace of God, we had chosen a time when the shadows from the setting sun had hidden us and some of the soldiers had left their post for their evening meal.

Although the soldiers were unaware of our presence, the nuns warned us to stay quiet and out of sight. We did as we were told.

Two days passed. We whispered among ourselves and with the nuns. No one knew what exactly was happening in Florence, and no one seemed to have any answers for our plight.

It was quite by accident that one of the German soldiers opened the door to our room. He said he was looking for Mother Superior but stopped cold when he spotted the four young women in the corner of the room. Without the nun's habits or veils, he immediately knew we were civilians. He said nothing. Leaning against the doorway, he slowly pulled a cigarette from his pocket. His eyes were focused on Stefanina. As he lit his cigarette, his gaze moved from the beautiful Italian and Arabic young woman to the rest of us—his grin was as unnerving as his stare.

One of the nuns hurriedly went to find Mother Superior. Within minutes, Mother Superior was eye to eye with the young soldier. *"No, no, no!"* She stated as she gently pushed him out of the room. *"Sono bambine!"* ("They are children!")

Frantically, Mother Superior came to us. "You must leave now!" She bent down to help us gather our few possessions. "The Germans know you are here. You are no longer safe!"

We quickly got our things and managed to stick a piece of bread in our pockets before we were escorted to a back entrance. "Go down the hill there." Mother Superior was pointing to a densely overgrown patch of trees and bushes. "You will find a path down to the main road. Do not stop! Do you understand?"

"Si, " we answered without hesitation.

The four of us cautiously climbed down the rugged path that evidently was known only to the nuns. Once we found the main road, we were careful not to wander out into the open. We sat together in silence under a tree. What were we to do? Where were we to go? We looked to Agnese. She must have felt the tremendous weight on her shoulders from the responsibility we had given to her. We needed her to tell us what we should do.

Stefanina got on her knees and began to pray, *"Ave Maria…."* ("Hail Mary….") It seemed like the only thing to do at the time. The rest of us got on our knees next to her and prayed to the Mother of God.

We prayed to God, His saints, and His angels. We prayed for guidance, for peace, for our families. We prayed to go home. Then we sat in silence.

Within a few minutes, Agnese lifted her head. She spoke with such confidence, I was sure God Himself had given her the answer to our dilemma. With as much courage as she could gather, Agnese told us her decision. "We must go back to Florence."

17

Nothing looked familiar as we tried to find our way back to Florence. The hills and valleys all looked the same to us. The roads were deserted; people had found refuge from the fighting. We had no protection, whether harm came in the form of Germans, thieves, or the elements, but we would not, could not, give up. We were four young women determined to find our way back into what could prove to be an even more dangerous situation than ever before.

I looked at my three friends. Agnese appeared so strong to me, but I could see the worry in her eyes. She pushed back a few strands of her red hair that had fallen over her face. She saw me watching her, and she smiled, "It will be all right Giovanna. We will find our way."

I held back the tears that would have given me some relief from the fear and concern I held inside. Since I had entered my teens, it seemed much more difficult for me to hold in my emotions. I thought of it as a weakness in my character, and it made me very angry with myself. I had no idea that this "weakness" was somehow related to my monthly visitor.

Stefanina and Carmela must have sensed my sadness and came over to me. Agnese followed. *"Giovanna, non ti preoccupare,"* ("don't worry") Stefanina said reassuringly as she put her arms around me. The other two joined in on the embrace. I felt so close to them at that moment; I had never felt that way before. *"Dio é con noi,"* ("God is with us") said Stefanina, "He will get us home safely." My tears flowed like a river!

As we walked down the unfamiliar roads of the countryside, we said nothing. Our hope was that we were heading towards the city. At times we hid in the bushes to rest, but never for more than a few minutes. The days were long, and we had only a few scraps of bread we had managed to put in our pockets before leaving the convent on the hill. An occasional brook quenched our thirst and allowed us to bath our sunburned faces. The hot August sun drained our young bodies of energy, but we knew we had to go on.

We heard the German soldiers before we saw them. Quickly we hid in the shrubbery as we decided our best course of action. Stefanina ripped a strip of cloth from her underskirt, and wrapped it around Carmela's arm. "Act as though you are hurt," she said. Stefanina and I embraced Carmela as we pretended to help her walk. Agnese slowly approached one of the German soldiers. Immediately he went for his weapon. Agnese lifted her arms. "I have no weapon," she said nervously. "Please," she begged in her best German, "may I speak to someone in charge?"

With a look of relief that we had not been the enemy who had caught him by surprise, the young man looked over at the rest of us, then back at Agnese. "What do you want?" he said as he lowered his pistol.

Agnese pointed to us. "We are trying to find our way back to our convent in the city. My friend is hurt, and we need to get help for her. Can you tell us the way back to *Ponte alla Carraia*? The convent is on the other side of the river."

"The bridges have been destroyed," said the soldier with a chuckle, "but the river is that way." He pointed in the general direction that we had been heading. *"Signorina,"* he added, "if you or your friends tell anyone where we are…." He slowly ran his hand across his throat. The message was clear.

Gunfire and cannon blasts could be heard as we approached the city of Florence. My heart raced as we ran for cover against the stone wall of a building. The four of us crouched down and huddled together; we were too scared to cry. We could see German soldiers running from building to building with their guns in hand. Bullets zinged by us, some so close I thought I could actually feel them fly by my head as they penetrated and shattered the wall in front of us. Then I saw, for the first time in my life, an American soldier. He was a black man. For a few seconds, my mind was in total confusion. The only black men I had ever seen had been Arabs in Tripoli; I wondered why the Arabs had come. There was no time to ponder, we were caught in the crossfire and had to run for our lives.

We knew that *Ponte Vecchio* was protected under the Geneva Convention, and we hoped we would be able to cross the Arno River there. To our disbelief, although the bridge was intact, the Germans had bombed both banks of the bridge making it impossible to access. There had to be a way across the river. We continued down the banks of the river asking other Italians in the streets for information. "Where do we cross? Is it safe?" Agnese inquired as we continued our search for a crossing. We were told that the Americans had now occupied the city and had spanned the river with makeshift bridges. We had hope, that is, until we saw what we had to do to get to the other side of the river.

I held on to the ropes for dear life as the bridge the Americans had provided swayed back and forth. It was then and there I discovered my fear of heights. The Arno never looked so dark and deep, and so far down! Now I felt I might really fall into the river and die. How ironic I thought. All the bullets I had escaped, just to drown in the Arno River!

18

After nearly a week of complete terror, we found our way back to the safety of our convent. Only two nuns had made their way back before us, and we all rejoiced and prayed for the safe return of the others. That night I jumped into my bed and hugged the sheets as if they were a long-lost relative. We were all exhausted and there was no energy left for the girlish conversations we so enjoyed before those past few weeks. With only my own thoughts and silent prayers of gratitude for our safe return, I soon fell into a deep sleep.

The explosion shattered our windows! Startled and confused, I jumped out of my bed just as the wall beside my bed began to crumble. For a moment, I thought I was dreaming. Was I in Naples about to be buried underground? Then, to my disbelief, I realized where I was. The blasts and explosions deafened my ears! I screamed out for the others, "Agnese! Carmela!" There was no answer. It was pitch dark as I crawled through the rubble towards the door. Once outside my room, I took a deep breath of air into my aching lungs—the crumbling stone wall had made it difficult to breathe. I ran through the gardens to the main convent building. Windows were shattering all around me! I kept running as bullets whistled by my head! Finally, I stumbled through the back door. *"Aiuto,"* ("Help") I screamed. I was trembling and sobbing uncontrollably. I knew that my friends had been injured or killed and might be lying under the rubble of our room.

"Giovanna! Giovanna are you hurt?" Several nuns ran to my side. "The others," I cried, "we must get to the others—they might be hurt…dead…help them!"

One of the nuns lifted me to my feet, "They are safe Giovanna. They are here." The other three girls had somehow made it out of our disintegrating building as well. They too had thought I had been buried under the fallen wall of our room and had come to the main building for help.

"Why did you leave me?" I shouted at them.

Agnese put her arms around me. "No Giovanna! We screamed out your name, but you did not answer; we couldn't see that anything was left but a pile of stone. We had to come for help! I am sorry—oh, my God," she cried. "I am so sorry! We would never intentionally leave you."

There was no time to understand what had happened, no time to think about our injuries; we all had to run for cover in the rooms below the convent.

To our sorrow, we realized the fighting was not over in Florence. For the next few nights, we hid in the catacombs under the church. We were not alone. Many who had come to the church for refuge were directed to go below. Lying or sitting on crowded blankets on the floor of the large underground room, women, children, and men of all ages waited for word from the priests that it was safe to return home.

Our small group of nuns and the four young women from Tripoli shared a tiny space together. Whispered prayers to God could be heard from all corners of the room. People joined in to say the Rosary and the Our Father. Eventually, after hours of prayer, the voices began to fade, and the room fell silent.

As we waited out the night, I looked around the room. People were bringing in an injured partisan. Perhaps he was already dead, but it was easier on my mind to think he was not. They lay him in the farthest corner of the room away from the women and children. I couldn't hear any moans or cries from the victim, but instead the eerie silence seemed to penetrate my ears as I stared at the ceiling above me—waiting for the explosion that would bury us alive.

Many people had fallen asleep in the arms of others. Children slept under the vigilant eyes of their parents, and many others did not sleep at all as they listened for any sign of danger infiltrating our safety.

I thought about the explosion that had destroyed my room several days before and had nearly taken my life—I shivered. I had brushed away the dust and particles of plaster and rock that had fallen on me when the bedroom wall had collapsed, and had suffered only a few scratches and bruises. How many times could I cheat death? Perhaps, I thought, I was akin to a cat with nine lives. I hoped that was the case. I needed to stay alive for Guido. My baby brother was waiting in Naples for me to take us home.

In a corner of the room, only feet from where I was sitting, I saw a young priest sitting with his head turned close to the ground as if he were listening to something. He spotted me looking at him and motioned me over. I looked around. My friends and the nuns had all fallen asleep. No one else seemed to have noticed him. Slowly I got up from the blanket—trying not to awaken the others, and I made my way toward the young priest. "What is your name," he asked.

"Giovanna Bonifazio," I answered quite proudly.

"Listen, Giovanna Bonifazio," he whispered with amusement, "the Americans are winning the war. Soon you will be able to go home. Where is your home?"

I stared at him. He was younger than I had originally thought, probably only a few years older than I was. "I am from Tripoli," I answered. "May I listen to the radio?"

"Yes, of course," he replied, "but keep it hidden. We can't take the chance that someone in this room might be spying on us!"

His name was Friar Malchizedek. He told me his name was from the Old Testament. "It means King of Righteousness," he explained. As we talked, I learned that he was still studying to become a priest.

As he spoke, I thought of the time in Naples a few years before, when the other girls in the convent and I would play a young girl's fantasy game of claiming any new young priest for ourselves. We need only be the first to proclaim, "I saw him first! He's mine!" The thought brought a smile to my face.

Friar Malchizedek was very nice looking, and very nice to talk to. Had it been under any other circumstance, I might have enjoyed a conversation with someone nearly my age and of the opposite sex. I had not had an intellectual conversation with a male in a long, long time. But now, hiding from the cannon fire above, my only thoughts were in his words of hope. "The war will soon be over, and you will be able to go home to Tripoli!" I missed my mother and brother so much. The mere possibility of being reunited with my family was almost too much for me to hope for.

For the next few nights, while others slept away the hours, Friar Malchizedek and I would sit together to listen to any news broadcast we could find on the radio and talk. He seemed interested in my ideas and thoughts, of my background, and my longing for my family. I almost looked forward to hiding beneath the church.

Once the Americans took control of the city, and we no longer had to hide in the catacombs, life in the convent returned to normal. But I was not to escape another loss in my life.

A young altar boy handed me the note and then ran away. I quickly unfolded the piece of paper. The message was hand written and seemed to have been jotted down in a hurry. *"Cara Giovanna,"* it began, "please meet me in the Sacristy after evening Mass. I have something of utmost importance to tell you." It was signed, Fra. Malchizedek. I could not imagine why he was summoning me.

The young Friar was already waiting for me when I entered the room. "You wanted to see me?" I asked.

There was sadness in his eyes as he approached. He stood very close to me—it felt awkward. "Giovanna," he began, "I wanted to say goodbye. I am leaving Florence."

I was confused. "But I thought you were going to stay here to become a priest! Why are you going? I don't understand." I was more surprised at my reaction to his announcement than I cared to admit. "I mean...."

He took my hands in his, "Shhh Giovanna. I don't want to go; I am being sent away. It is best," he said. "Please forgive me if I have caused you any problems."

Before I could get another word out of my mouth, he pulled me to him. He kissed me softly; his lips lingered for just a moment. As he backed away from me, the shock must have shone on my face as my mouth dropped open. There were tears in his eyes as he turned and hurriedly walked away.

I had no idea of the problems he was referring to, but I was too stunned to speak! There was nothing for me to do or say as I watched him leave. I never saw or heard from him again, but I shall always remember that my first kiss had been a bewildering surprise, in the house of God, and from a man of God.

After Friar Malchizedek left Florence, I learned that his superiors had seen us together in the catacombs and thought that the young man had shown too much interest in me. For his own good and mine, I was told, he was sent away to reconsider his choice of vocation before he took his final vows for the priesthood.

My young heart had felt a strange kind of pain and loss with the departure of my new friend. I had discovered a new feeling unlike any other I had experienced, but it was not to be the last time this door to my heart would open and shut.

There was surprisingly little damage to the city compared to the destruction that had befallen Naples. Finally, the Americans had taken over Florence and the streets were quiet again.

I still feared and dreaded the makeshift bridges that I was forced to cross each day to attend class, but I managed to cross them without falling into the Arno River and drowning. Sometimes on my way to and from school, I would pass a building or cafe, and I could hear loud music and laughter coming from inside. They were mainly the voices of American soldiers and Italian women. It always seemed like a celebration and many times they played American songs. I came to recognize what the Americans called the "jitter-bug." It was a very catching tune I thought, and the dance moves seemed to be so much fun. In the same instance, I couldn't help being appalled at knowing that Italian girls, victims of war the same as I, could so quickly befriend those that only months before had been the enemy. It was common knowledge that if any Italian girl was caught with the Americans, Italian boys and men would find them and shave their heads. It was a mark of shame for all to see.

19

In April of 1945, partisans captured and shot Mussolini and his mistress Clara Petacci. The next day, their bodies were taken to Milan and hung upside down from lampposts. A few days later, all German forces surrendered in Italy. It was time to go home, or so I had hoped. Unfortunately I was wrong. The Mediterranean Sea was inundated with mines and passenger ships were not yet able to cross to North Africa.

With my disappointment came unexpected news. My mother's cousin Selma, who lived in the nearby city of Bologna, had sent word to the convent that she and her family were coming to Florence to take me home with them. It was a bittersweet moment for me. I loved Florence, but I was ready to be with family—any family. I had never met Selma, but I knew of her. She was another Jewish woman who had married an Italian Catholic man. She too had married very well. Her husband was a Count, and they lived in a spectacular villa in Bologna. They had three sons, third cousins to me: Giulio, Giovanni, and Sandro. My cousins were very handsome young men who worked in their father's perfume business. During the war, they were forced to move their work to the basement of their villa.

It did not take me long to become one of the family. I worked in the basement with my cousins packaging the perfumes for shipment. In the evenings, we would enjoy our supper of homemade pasta or other delicious foods at a beautifully set table, and I would listen to the men talk of the war, politics and soccer. Sometimes they would ask my opinion about something—I think just for the sake of politeness and my answers seemed to impress them. After all, I had been studying intensely for the past five years and was well versed in most subjects.

Although the oldest boy, Giulio, was married, he spent little time with his wife. He insisted this was normal, and I should not worry about her. "After all," he said, "how often does one have the opportunity to show off such a beautiful cousin?" He and his youngest brother, Sandro, who was engaged to be married, would take me to the city and to the theater. I had fallen in love with the operas when my parents took me to see *"Aida"* as a young girl. In my heart I longed to continue the voice and music lessons which I had begun in Florence. "One day," I thought, "that could be me singing that very aria!"

We sat at outdoor cafes to have our coffee. It was great fun and all so new to me, especially all the attention I was getting. I was nearly sixteen-years-old, and except for the short time I had spent with Friar Malchizedek, I had never really had any interaction with males since my father died.

My cousins were wonderful, but the women in their lives were openly displeased with me living at the villa. I had heard Giulio and his wife arguing from time to time, but I had no idea it was about me. It was not until the day I walked in on Giulio and Sandro, who seemed to be on the brink of a fist fight, that I realized what was happening. "You are married; you should leave Giovanna alone," yelled Sandro. "Go home to your wife!"

"You only want her for yourself little brother," shouted Giulio. "Don't forget, you are to be married as well! Why don't you leave her alone?" There was more shouting and pushing but I was frightened and fled upstairs before the brothers ever knew I was there.

Selma saw me crying, "What is it Giovanna?" she asked as she lifted my face up to her. She was truly concerned, but I was so terrified, confused, and ashamed that all I could say was, "Giulio and Sandro are fighting!" I think she knew what was happening. Perhaps Giovanni, the middle son, had told her. He had made remarks to his brothers in the past that I had not understood until that very moment.

Selma held me while I cried. She whispered Hebrew words of reassurance to me which brought more tears. I hadn't heard those words since my mother had held me in her arms so many years before.

Days later, it was decided that I should return to Naples. "The mine fields will soon be cleared and you and Guido will be able to return to Tripoli," Selma explained. I said nothing. I knew the truth but was powerless in decisions pertaining to my own fate. Giulio and Sandro, however, were very vocal with their parents, insisting that it was not right that they send me away.

My uncle accompanied me to the train station and saw me board before he left. Shortly after, I saw Giulio running down the side of the train, frantically looking in all the windows as he passed. The train began to move just as he found me. "Giovanna," he screamed. "Get off! Please, get off!" He ran along the side of the train like a mad man.

I said nothing as tears streamed down my cheeks—tears of pain, of shame, and mostly of confusion. Giulio kept up with the train as long as he could, pleading with me all the while as it slowly left the station. "Please Giovanna, I will rent an apartment for you! You will want for nothing! Please just say you will get off at the next station, and I will meet you!"

I sat down and shook my head back and forth. "Goodbye, Giulio," I whispered to myself, "I just want to go home...."

20

Guido ran and jumped into my arms as I arrived at the castle in Arenella. He was eight-years-old but still very small for his age. Neither one of us was destined to be tall like our mother. We had so much to say, to talk about, yet we were content to hold each other. I had been unsure if my little brother would remember me, but his tight embrace eased my fears.

There were no other girls at the convent now, just me. I had been the only one of all the girls that had first come to Naples to be returned to the convent at Arenella. Fortunately, my godmother, Fiorenza D'Amelio, had moved to a small apartment built onto the newer section of the old castle, and I was sent to live with her. She welcomed me with open arms. I had forgotten how kind and loving she was.

"Giovanna, you have grown into a beautiful young woman," she said. "Have you been keeping up with your studies?"

"*Si, Madrina,*" ("Godmother") I replied, "I have done very well in my studies. But," I added, "I missed a lot of school when the fighting began in Florence and during the time I spent in Bologna." I had guessed that in total I was nearly a year behind in my studies.

She smiled at me and took my hand, "Well young woman, we must put you to work immediately. You must not fall behind in your studies." And she did. For one solid month, I studied day and night. Every evening, Sister Renata, who remained my favorite and most trusted friend, would bring me a candle to study by and a warm cup of *caffè latte* (coffee with milk). The coffee, of course, was to help me stay awake. Sometimes I would take a short break and go out onto my *madrina's* beautiful veranda. From this place, I had a panoramic view of Naples, Arenella and Mount Vesuvius. Once I even saw a new mouth of red flame coming from midway down the side of the volcano. It caused quite a stir and was news the next day. I wanted to believe that I had been the first to discover it.

In one month, I had easily caught up with the studies I had missed. My godmother did not act surprised, and I could tell she was very proud of me.

One night, as I studied by the light of the candle, *Madrina* entered my room with a plate of cookies. "I thought you might like a little something to go with your *caffè latte*," she said.

I unconsciously rubbed my eyes with my fists; nothing seemed to clear the fog that seemed to have settled over my vision. The simple act did not escape my godmother. She had already noticed that while I studied, I squinted and rubbed my eyes. "Giovanna," she said as she placed the plate on the nightstand, "are you having trouble seeing?"

"A little," I answered as I practically inhaled a cookie. "It is mostly at night and when I read…and actually, in the daytime too. I think I am just tired. I have been studying so hard to catch up."

Madrina held my face between her hands and kissed me on my forehead. "We will see the doctor tomorrow." A week later, I was the proud owner of my first pair of glasses. How amazing it was to see so clearly!

Now it was time for me to attend the schools in Naples. My grades were excellent—all except one. "Giovanna, what is this?" *Signora* D'Amelio asked as she looked at my school report. "You are failing your English class!"

"I am sorry *Madrina*," I replied, "but I find the language repulsive and offensive! I don't want to learn it!"

She took me by my hand and sat me down on the sofa next to her. This was not the first time my godmother had to sit me down and explain to me why I should or should not do something. It was as though she actually admired my stubbornness and occasional rebellious spirit, and she knew she had to get in touch with my intellectual side. "*Cara* Giovanna" she began, "do you want to go to the university?"

"Oh yes," I replied, "more than anything."

"Then you will have to do well in all your classes, including English! If not, I will not send you to the university. Do you understand?" She gave me a time limit in which to pull up my grade in the loathed subject.

My next report was of no surprise to her. I excelled in all my subjects, including English. "There is nothing difficult about the language," I told her, "any idiot could learn it!"

21

The sisters at the convent were busy trying to put their lives back together again, as well as the lives of the children who had been there for nearly seven years. The war was over, but the struggle to survive was not.

Many people waited for the passenger ships to sail once again across the Mediterranean Sea. All the children needed to be reunited with their families, as did many other Italians who had escaped Tripoli in 1940 with the mistaken idea that Africa would be the only center of conflict.

American military ships docked in the port of Naples gave many locals the opportunity to sell their meager goods to the sailors onboard. The sailors were particularly generous to the Neapolitan children who asked for coins and candy.

The sisters at the convent found these ships to be a profitable market for their handmade embroidered linens. The money was badly needed at the convent which still housed the refugee children of Tripoli.

For safety, the nuns always went to the city in pairs. On one particular day, Sister Renata was one of the nuns going to the American ship. I thought, "This is my chance!" I cornered my friend as she gathered her goods.

"*Suor Renata,*" I began in my sweetest of voices, "that is so much for you to have to carry. I could help you if you would like."

I saw the edges of her lips curl up, but she caught herself before she smiled. My friend looked over at me with a very serious stare! "Do you think I am unable to carry these items by myself? Do you think me old? Frail?"

I smiled my most endearing smile, "Of course you are not old! I just wanted to help you, that is all!"

Sister Renata put her hands on her hips. "Giovanna Bonifazio, do you mean to tell me you only want to help me? Could it be you want to see the ship? Perhaps talk a sailor out of some candy? Don't lie!"

"How can you...." I stopped myself. I had never been able to fool Sister Renata; she was always three steps ahead of me! "*Si,*" I admitted, "I do want to go to the ship. Can I please?"

"Finally the truth, huh? It is not up to me. If *Suor* Maria says it is alright, then you can come. I will ask her."

I was so excited. I was sure Sister Maria would allow me to go with the two of them. Just the thought of doing something out of the normal daily routine was making me feel and act like a five-year-old!

The nuns and I were invited onboard with other merchants from the city. I tried not to seem too excited as I stepped on the ship's deck. Many sailors were already buying and bargaining with the locals for gifts to bring back to their families in America. Sister Renata and Sister Maria quickly opened their carefully wrapped packages of embroidered linens to show to the men. "Notice the fine embroidery," stated Sister Maria in very good English. "The money from these things will go to the children at the convent and to help the poor."

I stood next to the nuns as they very skillfully bartered for the best possible price for their linens. At first I thought someone had bumped into me, and for politeness sake, I did not turn around to avoid embarrassing anyone. Seconds later, I felt it again. This time someone had one of my thick braids in their hands! Stunned, I quickly turned around.

"*Bella!* (Beautiful!) Very pret-ty! *Ca-pish?*" ("Do you understand?") His attempts at Italian would have been amusing had he not had one of my braids in his hands—petting it as if it were a cat, and putting it to his nose!" "No!" I shouted as I reclaimed my braid. "No touch!"

The young sailor stepped toward me. "You speak English?" He seemed a bit excited!

"No, she no speak English," lied Sister Renata as she stepped in between the rambunctious young American and me. Sister Maria joined us, and the two of them formed a solid brick wall between me and my pursuer.

The young man held his hands up to his shoulders, palms forward, as if he were surrendering to the enemy. "No harm, *señorita!* Just being friendly—that's all." He hadn't realized he had switched to Spanish!

"She is only a baby!" declared Sister Maria. "You must not talk to her!"

The young sailor looked around the two nuns standing shoulder to shoulder. "<u>That</u> is no baby! Look," he added, "if you bring her back with you tomorrow, I will buy all your stuff!"

"Not is 'stuff'," stated Sister Renata, "is very fine linen!"

"Okay, okay, fine linen—I will buy it all! Just bring her with you!"

The nuns were speechless. They each grabbed one of my arms, and all but dragged me off of the ship. The scene had drawn the attention of many of the men on the deck. I dared not turn around to see the young sailors calling after me, "Come back! *Bella*—I have candy!"

My embarrassment was only outdone by the anger of the nuns. "Do not look back Giovanna," they commanded.

Needless to say, that was my last trip to the docks with the nuns. The events of that day brought about a new realization for me. I was no longer a little girl; no longer could I hide behind the ideals of the convent; I had feelings that could only be attributed to my blossoming womanhood.

Sister Renata had said, "Don't lie!" She was right! I could not lie to myself, but instead I had to admit the attention I had gotten on that ship was flattering, as well as embarrassing, and in truth, I had really enjoyed the attention given to me by the young American.

I knew without a doubt that I would never be a nun, even though I admired with all my heart and soul the work, love, and devotion the nuns had shown me for the past seven years. For the first time, I knew the things I wanted out of my life. I wanted a family. I wanted to teach. I wanted to sing. I never dreamed that I could not have all those things!

22

Each morning I walked down the hill from the castle to the bus stop on the main road. Usually I was alone, but occasionally, a local farmer or housewife would wait for the bus as well. Madrina saw to it that I had the correct change for the bus fare to school and back, and a nice *panino* (sandwich) and a piece of fruit for my lunch.

The ride to the moderately damaged school took us through several sections of Naples. Some parts were heavily damaged by the bombing, and other parts seemed to have escaped the devil himself.

On one of the buildings I spotted a huge banner draped on the side of a wall. The sign advertised a new cinema—an American musical being shown in town. I strained my neck as I attempted to read the banner from the moving bus. "The Follies," I read. I remember hearing about them in Bologna. I missed the outings with my cousins Sandro and Giulio, especially the ones to the cinemas and operas.

I felt certain that *Madrina* would never allow me to go to a cinema. Money was scarce, and my time was better spent engulfed in my studies. Then, from somewhere in my subdued mischievous brain, an idea began to form. "The bus fare! I could walk to school for a couple of days, and I would have enough money to see the film!"

For several days, I got up earlier than usual and walked to school using short-cuts through the village. Within a few days, I had enough money saved in order to see the musical, and I did the unthinkable—I skipped class.

Whatever guilt I should have been feeling was overshadowed by the extreme excitement and anticipation I was experiencing while I patiently waited for the cinema house to open. I bought my ticket and entered the building. So far, no one I knew had seen me, and I felt certain no one would see me once inside the movie theater.

I took a seat in an empty aisle—I felt so grown up! The room darkened as the images began to appear on the screen. I was so captivated with the singing and dancing before me, that I did not notice the person who had taken a seat next to me.

The strange hand on my knee caused me to freeze in fear. In my paralyzed state, I couldn't make myself look over at my molester. It could have been a male or a female, I would never know. The hand began to travel up my leg and between my thighs. I gasped, grabbed the hand and pushed it to the side. Quickly, I gathered my books and ran out of the building and for a block down the street. I wanted to cry, but I dared not bring attention to myself and have someone tell Mother Superior, or worse yet, Madrina, that I had skipped class.

I wandered aimlessly for a while before I was calm enough to ask someone for the time. To my dismay, I had hours to wait before the bus would arrive at the stop on the road below the castle. I couldn't just return to the convent early, someone would certainly notice. It was just a small error in my strategic planning for the forbidden outing. As if for punishment, I entered a nearby church and was forced to wait for several hours as I pondered on my stupidity.

Weeks passed and I all but forgot the incident at the cinema. No one was the wiser. Each day I followed my routine of catching the bus to and from my school. To wait for the return bus to the convent, I waited in the *piazza* near the school. The *piazza* was always bustling with the comings and goings of the locals, as well as soldiers from various allied countries. It wasn't uncommon to see the less desirable class of people in the area as well. I found watching and analyzing people a rather amusing pastime while I waited for my bus.

It was while I was busy thinking about some stranger I had spotted in the *piazza*—perhaps inventing a story about their life, when a jeep full of men pulled up in front of me at the bus stop. Suddenly, some of the people in the *piazza* began to run as they screamed *"Mamma, Pappa!"* I had no idea what was happening, but my first inclination was to run as well. Then without warning, the men jumped out of their jeep and grabbed me. It suddenly came to me—these men were Italian and American military police. *"Mamma, Pappa,"* was the street code for military police. I screamed at the top of my lungs, *"Aiuto!"* ("Help!")

The Italian soldiers held me tighter and ordered me to shut up. I kicked and screamed even louder as I tried with all my might to escape from my abductors. I threatened to have Mother Superior take their heads off when she found out about what they were doing. It was useless; I wasn't going to get away!

Minutes later the jeep stopped in front of a building that I did not recognize. As I still kicked and screamed, two of the soldiers dragged me inside. I noticed men behind bars as we passed through the narrow hallway. The prisoners shouted out obscenities in German at the passing soldiers. Fear flooded my body—I became limp and mute!

"Why was I going to jail? What had I done?" My thoughts were chasing each other in my mind. The soldiers dragged me into a small, poorly lit room where I was forced to lie down on a filthy bed. I tried to get up, but one of them pushed me back down. Suddenly, I found my voice once again. "I live at the convent in Arenella! Please get Mother Superior! There has been a terrible mistake!"

The soldier standing by the door began to laugh, "Very clever," he said. "She dresses like a schoolgirl and knows the names of the nuns! Ha, is that the way you entice the soldiers—take them for all their money?"

The soldier that was holding me down seemed to give his cohort a questioning look. The third soldier left the room. I heard them say something about a doctor. Then someone else talked about an examination. "We'll see if she's a schoolgirl or a common street whore!"

"What am I hearing?" I thought. I knew that many young women had taken to the streets in order to feed their families, but how could the soldiers have mistaken me for one? Terror seized my soul! "They can't possibly think that I am….!" The idea was so ridiculous; I couldn't even fathom the thought! Again I began screaming out the name of the convent and of Mother Superior!

"If I let you go," said the American soldier, "will you promise to stop screaming?"

"*Sì!* I mean, yes, I promise. Please," I begged, "you must believe me. Please sir, just get Mother Superior!"

The American got up and allowed me to sit on the side of the bed while he took his partner to the doorway. I could not hear all that they were saying, but I knew it had to do with the convent. Seconds later, one of the men left, while the other sat in a chair by the bed. I dared not say anymore as I wiped away the tears from my eyes.

What seemed an eternity later, I heard Mother Superior's angry voice bellowing through the hall. "Where is Giovanna? I demand to see Giovanna! You better not have harmed a hair on her head! You will all suffer the consequences if that child has been harmed!"

I had never heard Mother Superior raise her voice, but now, her presence was surely known in that building. Immediately, I jumped off the bed as the stunned soldier pushed his chair to the side to let me by. Mother Superior muffled a scream as she entered the room and saw the bed where I had been held. She held out her arms as I ran into her embrace. "Giovanna," she cried, "my poor little girl!"

Once back at the safety of the convent, Madrina and Mother Superior both questioned me about the actions of the soldiers. Without coming right out and saying it, they were most concerned that I might have been sexually molested. Their sighs of relief from my answers confused me at that time. I did not quite understand what it was the soldiers didn't do to me, and puzzled that my mental anguish over the events was not as horrible an outcome. I was even more confused than ever! Although I was not physically hurt, I cried for hours. The incident was never mentioned again, and I dared not ask what consequences befell my abductors.

23

After the forbidden outing to the cinema and the arrest by the military police, I was more appreciative of the convent's restrictions, and I prayed that God would forgive my youthful indiscretions.

All that resided at the convent still attended Mass early every morning, but Sunday Mass was special. The sweet voices of the all boys' choir resounded through the chapel every Sunday morning. I had sung in the choir for almost five years, but now, as I listened to the boys, I closed my eyes and envisioned angels singing in the clouds. Their sweet little voices gripped my heart. Guido stood side-by-side with his schoolmates. His little altar boy robe seemed to swallow up his tiny body. I knew that my little brother did not have the gift for singing that I had, but he and his slightly off key voice were too adorable to ignore. As he sang, his eyes searched the pews for me. Once our vision connected, he would give me a huge boyish grin while still trying to maintain his composure and poise.

There was precious little time to spend doing anything except schoolwork, chores, and prayers. Occasionally Guido, or *Guiduccio* as I liked to call him, and I managed to find time alone beneath one of the tangerine trees in the orchard. I held him close to me and ran my fingers through his hair. *"Guiduccio,"* I said, "soon we will go home to Tripoli. Do you remember Tripoli? Do you remember *Mamma?*"

He would turn his head up and stare at me with his big brown eyes, "I don't remember anything Giovanna...was there a boat?"

"Si, tesoro, ("treasure") we came to Italy in a very big boat. Soon the ships will be able to sail again, and you and I will be on the very first one. What do you think about that?"

He fell silent and in deep thought. His little shoulders sunk forward, and he let out a long sigh. "Giovanna," he turned to look at me, "can't this be our home?" This convent had been all he really knew. Papa had died when he was two, and our mother had been in the hospital since he was a few months old.

"Guido, Guido, Guido," I laughed and jumped to my feet, "don't tell me you want to become a priest or a brother? Let me see—*Padre* Guido Bonifazio! No, no! How about Sister Guido? Would you like that?" He sprang to his feet and chased me around the orchard, past the courtyard and out onto the grass outside the convent. "*Padre* Guido, *Padre* Guido!" I let him catch me, and we laughed like fools as we both fell to the ground. We lay side by side facing the sky.

"Giovanna, will the planes return?"

"*No, Guiduccio,*" I replied, "the planes are gone for good! We are safe now." I turned to look at him and ran my fingers through his hair again. "Hey, you know what? I will give you a haircut so you will look nice when we get on the ship. Would you like that?"

"Can you cut hair?" he asked with a very puzzled look on his face.

"I can do anything I want to do my little brother! I would even shave you if you had two whiskers on your chin!" We laughed as we ran into the convent in search of scissors.

The next morning at Mass all the young boys took the front pews as always, and I found a seat directly behind my brother. There was much commotion and giggling among the boys as Guido rubbed the top of his head. He was enjoying all of the attention. Sister Renata looked over at me and could not hide her amusement. She knew! There was only one person who would be brave enough to do such a thing—Giovanna! I had given Guido his wish and cut a perfect circle of hair off the top of his head. Now he truly resembled a miniature *padre*!

24

I don't know how I did not notice my godmother's failing health. I must have thought her need to rest more often during the day was part of being old. She was still vigilant over my progress in school, and to me, that concern over my grades voided any doubts that I might have entertained about her well-being.

My seventeenth birthday came without much notice as well. Just one of many birthdays that was spent in the daily routines of the convent and school. By now, I had reached my full height of four feet and ten inches. It certainly was not what I had hoped for, but I knew I would have to deal with it. I consoled myself by thinking that my brain was most likely larger than normal!

With the exception of my height, my looks were of little concern to me; I still carried the strict teachings of the convent about vanity deeply rooted inside of me. Since the day on the American ship, I knew the way I looked was very appealing to men, but I tried to ignore the whistles or comments from men in the streets of Naples. Usually, the attention was embarrassing, and I did everything I could to avoid males—especially a group of them.

I still wore my thick auburn hair in braids that hung to my waist. The weight of the braids at times became so bothersome, that I was tempted to use the same pair of scissors I had used on Guido's hair to cut them off. The fear that the nuns might think I had lost my mind, or that I was plagued with vanity, kept me from carrying out the gruesome deed.

There was still no news about the ships sailing to or from Africa. I longed to be with my mother, but as yet, I had not heard any news from home. There were no thoughts in my mind that she may have died from the tuberculosis, and Guido and I might have been orphans. I had kept the image of her face in my mind for almost seven years, and I would fantasize about our reunion. I imagined she was totally cured and would meet Guido and me at the docks in Tripoli with her arms outstretched, ready to reclaim her children. She would look as grand as she did when Papa was alive—with her beautiful black hair fixed in the latest style. She would be dressed in a handsome linen suit—tailor-made of course. It was going to be so perfect. She might even have gifts for Guido and me. The fantasy had kept me strong all those years.

My godmother and the sisters at the convent were wonderful. They were my family until the day I would be reunited with my own people. Maybe I thought all my hardships and unhappiness were over when the war ended, and I returned to Arenella. I was sadly mistaken! Sadness and tragedy were not to escape me before I left Naples.

One day as I returned from school, Sister Renata met me at the entrance of the convent. "Giovanna, *cara* (dear) Giovanna," she began. I knew by the look on her face that something was terribly wrong. My first thoughts were of my brother.

"*Dov è Guido?*" ("Where is Guido?") I shouted as I threw down my books and pushed my way past her. Sister Renata caught me by the arm. *"Non è Guido,"* ("It's not Guido") she said calmly.

All the signs I had avoided seeing up to this moment, now came to me in a flood of realization. *"Madrina?"*

"Si, tesoro," she put her arms around me, "your godmother has died."

I began to sob uncontrollably, pleading with her to tell me it wasn't true. "But how, how could she die? Why?"

"Your *madrina* had cancer Giovanna. She didn't want you to worry about her, so she did all she could to hide the sickness from you. She loved you very much!" Renata continued to hold me as we walked to my godmother's apartment. I did not know what "cancer" meant—what it possibly could be; all I knew was that it meant death.

Madrina was lying in her bed, her gray hair neatly arranged on her pillow, and her delicate hands lying by her side. The curtains were drawn, and only the filtered rays of the setting sun lit the small room. Mother Superior was by her side, as were several of the nuns that I had come to know and love.

I leaned over and kissed my beloved *madrina*—the coldness of her skin brought on a new wave of sorrow and sobbing. As Sister Renata gently pulled me off of the body, she whispered reassurances to me, "She's with God now Giovanna."

My mind no longer saw what was present before me in that room. In an instant I was transported back to that ten-year-old little girl sitting by her father's body—willing him to breathe.

25

For days after my godmother's death and burial, the heavy odor of disinfectant the nuns had used to purge my godmother's room of disease, hung in the air. If cancer could be eradicated with the potent smelling chemical, then no one else was in any danger of contracting the deadly killer.

I wondered what would become of me now. My benefactor was gone, and any hopes of going to the university died with her. Whatever wealth she had was left to the convent. If she had provided for me before her death, no one had followed her wishes, and no one admitted to knowing of any such provisions. Now more than ever, I needed to get back to Tripoli.

The news of my mother's arrival in Naples came as a complete surprise and shock. It was January of 1947. When I heard she would be arriving on the next ship from Tripoli, I was totally dumbfounded. "Could my dreams be coming true?" I thought. "She must be well again to be able to travel to Italy to reclaim her children!"

My fantasy of our joyous reunion was soon crushed. The summons from Mother Superior no longer frightened me as they once did when I first came to the convent, but instead, I found the opportunity to talk with the head of the convent rather stimulating. "Sit down my child," instructed Mother Superior as she too took her seat behind her small, wooden desk. "Giovanna, I have news that your mother is on the ship that has just today docked in Naples."

I gasped, "The ship is here? My mother is here?"

"Yes, Giovanna," she said as she rose from her chair and came to stand in front of me. This act in itself was unnerving. I stood before her—looking up to see the pity in her eyes. My mind was racing with thoughts of my mother, of leaving Naples, and then—that there was something terribly wrong! My mouth dropped open, and I held my breath.

"Is she well? Is there something wrong Mother? I dared to ask.

"Your mother is not well Giovanna. She was taken directly to the hospital from the ship."

Huge puddles of tears began to form in my eyes. Within seconds the dam broke, and tears flowed like rivers down my face. Months of worry, sadness, and anguish finally found the reason to explode within my body. I trembled uncontrollably, and I cried like I never cried before—this time in the arms of Mother Superior.

I could only hope this was going to be just a minor setback for my mother, and she would be well enough to take us home in a few days. Mother Superior had not had word on the severity of my mother's condition.

Guido was playing with his friends when I motioned for him to come to me.

There was no need to go into any detail with my little brother. He would not have understood. Instead, I told him about our mother being in the city and of the wonderful reunion the three of us would have. Then, before he got too excited, I explained that she had to go to the hospital first because she did not feel well after the long trip. He did not know how to act or what to say about the news. I was sure he had no recollection of our mother. The only mothers he knew were the nuns at the convent. For him, the memories I tried to keep alive for the two of us was perhaps like me telling him a fairly tale that eventually would have a happy ending. Guido looked to me for a suitable reaction to the news of the arrival. He could tell I was not happy, but had no idea why.

"Giovanna," he said with concern, "we can stay here with the sisters if you want."

"No Guiduccio," I answered when I realized what he was thinking. "I <u>want</u> to see *Mamma*. I have missed her so much. It will be such a happy reunion—you will see!" His big brown eyes tried to see some truth in what I had said to him. "You will see," I repeated as I forced myself to smile.

Guido and I, accompanied by Sister Renata, approached Caldarelli Hospital with anticipation and fear of the unknown. What would we say to our sick mother? Would we recognize her? Would she recognize us?

Again the smell of disinfectant burned the insides of my nose as we walked down the halls of the hospital. I looked down at Guido. He was rubbing his eyes—the strong fumes were irritating them.

All around us we could hear the moaning of the sick and the dying, and the reassuring voices of the nuns attending to them. Guido and I walked as one, holding hands, unable to utter a single word to each other. His other hand tightly grasped the edge of Sister Renata's gown. Guido began to drag his feet as we walked down the unfamiliar halls. His little hand began to pull at the handful of cloth. Sister Renata finally stopped to release his hand from her clothes. "Do not be afraid Guido," she said as she took his tiny hand in hers.

The ward was large with rows of beds on either side. Only a flimsy piece of white cloth hung between the beds. Everything appeared to be white—sheets, blankets, nurses. Many patients were coughing and moaning and paid little attention to the visitors that had just entered their ward. Sister Renata whispered something to one of the nuns, and then turned in the direction the nun was pointing. I knew they were looking at the woman I once knew as my mother. She seemed smaller than I remembered—thin and emaciated. Perhaps, had the nuns not pointed her out, I would never have recognized her. Her once lustrous black hair was now lifeless and cropped short. Her cheekbones protruded, and her eyes seemed to have sunken into her head. *"Mamma?"* I reluctantly said her name. *"Mamma?"*

She stirred from her restless sleep and immediately began to cough. Her frail hand automatically reached for her handkerchief that was already tinged with bloody sputum. "Giovanna? Guido?" She reached out, and my brother and I ran into her arms. *"I miei bambini, i miei tesori! Non ci posso credere!"* ("My children, my treasures! I can't believe it!")

Immediately, a violent coughing spell came upon her, and she pushed us away. Between the coughing, the blood, and the gasping for air, she tried to tell us not to come near her. Her sobs were inaudible, but the tears flowed as if she had saved them all for that moment. Sister Renata kept us from going to her again. "She doesn't want you to get sick. You mustn't go too close to her."

So there we were—my beloved mother, my frightened little brother and I, standing just a few feet apart, crying out endearments, and longing for the embraces we so much needed from one another. Our hearts ached for the physical touch that was now being denied to us by the invisible wall of disease.

26

I knew I had to leave the convent. It was time. I could no longer fool myself into believing my mother would get well enough to travel back to Tripoli with Guido and me. We would have to return home alone. But first, I had to make the trip by myself to make arrangements for a place for us to live and to get a job to support us. I had no idea what I would do. I had no training in any profession, and I had not been able to go to the university to study to become a teacher. Fear of the unknown again clenched my heart—there was no other solution—I would have to return to Tripoli alone.

With tearful eyes, I said goodbye to my mother. I wanted so much to hold her and to be held by her, but the nuns would not allow it. I got as close as I could, *"Ti voglio tanto bene mamma, non preoccuparti per noi."* ("I love you very much mama, don't worry about us.") I stood for a moment outside her ward; I could hear her coughing and crying. For a moment, the desire to run back to her bedside and take her in my arms was overwhelming. I had to think of Guido. If I got sick, what would become of him? My heart ached with the pain I was feeling as I left my mother in that place. Every fiber of my being felt the pain. I could do nothing else but cry as I left the hospital ward for the last time.

Saying goodbye to Guido was no easier. He still had vivid memories of the last time I had left him to go with the nuns to Rovereto. *"Guiduccio,"* I reassured him, "I will find us a home, and you will be on the next ship to Tripoli. Don't be afraid."

As we held each other tightly he looked up at me. Tears flowed from his eyes. "I am scared Giovanna. What if something happens to you—like our *mamma*? I don't want to be alone. Please don't leave me!"

"No, no, my sweet little boy, I will always take care of you, nothing will happen to me. I am your big sister, and I will find us a home. Don't you worry!" I tried to sound as convincing as I could, but deep inside I was as scared as he was. *Suor* Renata took Guido by the hand as she kissed me goodbye. She was still my most trusted friend, and I relinquished the care of my brother to her safekeeping. *"Arrivederci,* Renata," I said with a grin on my face. I didn't realize at the time that I would never see her again.

"*Suor* Renata, Giovanna!" she corrected as she playfully swatted me on my bottom.

"*Si, si, Suor Renata,*" I replied, "I love you both!"

As I walked toward the ship, I smiled. I was glad that my playful exchange with Sister Renata had made Guido laugh. They were waving their arms and calling out my name as I again became part of the long line of people boarding a ship. It was March of 1947, six years and nine months since I had left my home.

Hundreds of Italians boarded the ship that day. Most of them seemed happy to be returning to Tripoli; some seemed anxious and worried about what was or was not awaiting them, and others, as I, were torn between fear and happiness. The things we had seen in Italy during the war, the destruction, the death, would forever leave a scar on our minds and hearts. Families had been torn apart; homes and fortunes had been lost—those things we all had in common. But the fact remained, those who had boarded the ship that day and in the months to follow had survived to tell their stories for generations to come.

Many of the Italians remained on the top deck. I gazed out over the sparkling emerald sea in reverent admiration. I wondered if the Mediterranean Sea was still "*Mare Nostrum,*" as Mussolini had called it. What did it matter anymore?

As the hours passed, many of the passengers on deck became acquainted—some even found old friends. Soon the voices of the solemn crowd became alive with Italian dialogue from all regions of Italy, and best of all, there was laughter. Singing and dancing followed naturally, as the mood became festive. We were nearing our home. Though I had never danced in public before, I found myself clapping and singing with the crowd. I felt the fear lift from my heart, for although I was alone, I was really part of this family—the family of survivors. I knew I would be alright. After all, I had been the little girl at the convent who volunteered to go upstairs to save a fellow student while the bombs dropped on Naples! I had all but frozen to death in Rovereto, and nearly crushed by the exploding wall in my bedroom in Florence. What could possibly happen to me that I had not already lived through? How many more cat lives did I have?

PART III
Return to Tripoli

27

I had no idea my brother Renzo would be waiting for me on the docks in Tripoli. He had not changed since I had last seen him—Renzo was as handsome as I remembered him. As I ran to him, the look of surprise on his face was apparent. He had dropped off a scrawny little girl at the convent seven years before, and now was watching a young woman run into his arms. He stared at me in disbelief as he too began to run towards me. "Giovanna, is it really you?" He picked me up with one giant swoop and swung me around. "Giovanna, Giovanna, Giovanna! I can't believe it is you!" He held me tightly as if I might escape.

"*Si,* Renzo, <u>it is</u> me!" I cried.

Renzo Bonifazio

During the ride to his home, we attempted to recall every moment of the past seven years—impossible to do of course. We were both too excited to stop talking. He told me he was married and had a baby son. What he failed to tell me was that his wife was unaware that he had a sister, and shocked when he told her to set another plate at the dinner table. "Wait until I tell her to set yet another plate when our little brother arrives," he laughed, and for a moment he reminded me so much of my father—our father!

Pina, my sister-in-law, did not seem amused at the discovery of additional family, and less than excited about Renzo's half-brother and sister staying with them in their apartment. Not wanting to be a burden on my brother and his family, I immediately set out to find work. I wanted and needed to provide for myself and my little brother who arrived just one week later. But first, I had to do something I had wanted to do for a long time. I had my first visit to a beauty shop.

The hairdresser looked at me in disbelief when I told him to cut off my hair. *"Ma no, signorina,"* He pleaded as he shook his head from side to side. "You have such beautiful hair—it would be a sin!"

"Signore," ("Sir") I answered, "I am old enough to know what I want! I want a short, stylish haircut like the American film stars. If you won't do it, I will just have to go elsewhere!"

My arrogance must have convinced him. *"Si,"* he admitted as he picked up his scissors, "it is your hair!" He hesitated for a moment, scissors poised by the side of my head. For a moment, as he looked me in the eyes through my reflection in the mirror, I thought he was not going to do it! Then he took a breath, held one of my thick auburn braids in his hand, and began to cut. It took several snips to sever away seven years of my childhood. The relief from having all that weight taken off my head was mixed with the sadness of parting with something that had been my constant companion for all those years!

Now there was only one other thing I knew I had to do—I needed to see the *palazzina* just one more time. In my heart and mind, there was something of my childhood left behind those walls—some small part of Giovanna I needed to reconnect with to make me whole again. I had left most of my happy memories in that house, and I needed closure to that part of my life.

A Jewish family had bought the *palazzina* from my father when he had to declare bankruptcy. I slowly approached the huge oak doors and knocked. *"Buon giorno,"* ("Good day") I said shyly as the owners of the house opened the door. "My name is Giovanna Bonifazio."

Although reluctant to open their doors to a stranger in times of Jewish persecution, they listened to my story and allowed me to enter. They remembered my father and mother. "They were such a nice couple," they said. "We know it must have been difficult for them to sell us their home."

I followed behind the new owners as they showed me the few changes they had made to the house—my house! My mind drifted back to my childhood within those walls. I could see my father and Enrico sitting on the sofa under the clock on the wall (although the room was decorated differently now). I heard *Mamma* calling *Ciccio* for dinner, and Papa searching for the chameleons. I could see myself on Papa's lap searching through his vest pockets for my surprise. And then, at the top of the stairs, I saw the door. The stained glass had been replaced—it was whole again.

One of the new owner's sons came in just as I was about to leave. I was introduced to him with a short history. "Giovanna!" He exclaimed. "Could it be?" He took my hand as if he had known me all of his life and led me to the garage. There, as if nothing had ever changed, was the Ballila with my name still on the tag! It was almost too much for me to bear, and I fought to hold back the tears. I was relieved that the young man was oblivious to my emotions. He was excited to finally meet the "Giovanna" that adorned the license plate on his car, and he insisted on driving me around the city. It was not what I had imagined as a small girl with her father.

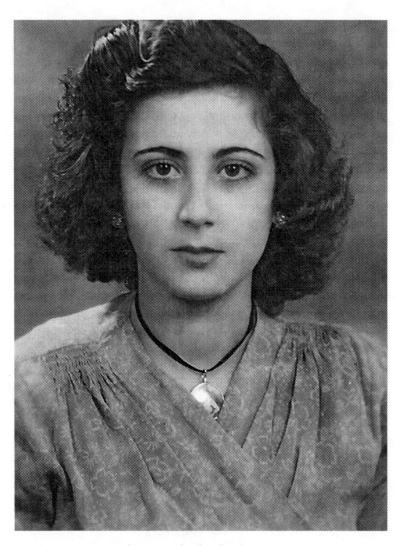

Giovanna after her first haircut.
1947

28

My search for work began with my mother's relatives. I had hoped that with so many Jewish relatives still in the city, someone would have a shop or grocery store that needed hired help. I wasn't concerned with the type of work; at this point, I was willing to do almost anything to support my little brother and myself.

It was a bittersweet moment when I was reunited with my mother's family. There were so many happy memories and so many tragic ones as well, and there was one essential and important person missing from this reunion—my mother.

I was told that one of my cousins owned a shoe store in the city—possibly he could use the help. The thought of working around beautiful new shoes was certainly not anything I would mind. I loved shoes, although I had not owned new shoes since I left Tripoli. My feet were so small; I could only hope that one day I would be able to wear elegant women's shoes.

I stopped in front of the shoe shop before entering. A pair of brown leather shoes displayed in the front window caught my attention. They had just a small heel and a strap over the instep. I sighed. I knew it was only wishful thinking—I couldn't even afford rent, much less a pair of new leather shoes.

After introducing myself and explaining the way in which we were related, I asked my cousin if he needed help in his shop. "Unfortunately," he said, "I am not in need of another person. But," he added, "if you would like to come in and work for a few days, I will give you that pair of shoes you were admiring in the window."

My heart leaped with joy. Although I knew shoes would not pay the rent, I agreed to work for a few days. I rationalized that I could use a nice pair of shoes for subsequent job interviews, and I needed the work experience.

I arrived early to work the very next morning. Immediately I began sweeping the floors and dusting the shelves. The smell of leather was intoxicating—I found myself taking in deep breaths of the rich aroma as I worked. I think I must have fondled every pair of shoes in the store. As I worked and became comfortable with my employer and the surroundings, I unconsciously began to sing as I went about my duties. It began with a soft hum, then, when my cousin was away on an errand, I burst into full song! One day, soon after my cousin had stepped out of the store, a man entered the shop. "May I help you sir?" I could feel the blood rushing to my face from the embarrassment of having a customer hear me sing. He was looking around the store as if there might be someone else in the room he wanted to speak to. "Sir," I said, "are you looking for the owner?"

"Was that you singing?" He asked, as he continued searching for the other non-existent person.

I again blushed a thousand colors of red. "Yes sir," I reluctantly admitted.

He looked at me as if he were trying to picture the voice coming from this tiny Italian girl. "You are quite good," he finally said.

"Oh, thank you sir! I love to sing, but I am not very good at it!"

He shook his head, "You are—you are very good. Would you be interested in singing at the cinema?"

"Sir?" I had no idea what he was referring to. He explained that during intermission at the cinema house, he hired added entertainment for the patrons' enjoyment while they waited for the second half of the movie to begin.

"You would be paid, of course." He added.

I could actually do what I loved to do for pay; I could hardly believe what I was hearing. Amazing. "Okay!" I replied in English to the Italian gentleman.

Renzo was excited for me, but reluctant to let his little sister go alone. "Giovanna," stated Renzo as he grabbed his hat, "I am going—no need to argue. I do not know this man, and neither do you! I will not allow you to go without me!"

Pina was understanding. "She's a grown woman Renzo," she said without hesitation. "Let her go."

Renzo looked at his wife and his son in her arms, but said nothing. He gave them both a brief kiss and followed me out of the apartment.

Once on the stage, I peeked around the curtain; the room was full. Excitement and fear radiated through my body. I had sung for many years as part of church choirs, but never before with so many people—complete strangers watching and listening. This was nothing like the choir; I was the main attraction and alone on the stage.

"O Sole Mio...." To my delight, the audience clapped and cheered, and I had barely begun. Their encouragement was all that I needed. I sang my heart out to them!

What an extraordinary night! I couldn't have felt any more excited if I had been the star of an opera, singing her aria in the magnificent theaters of Florence. Even more exciting was being asked to return to sing again on another night.

Renzo was dumbfounded. He had no idea I could sing. "Mamma mia," he stated with pride, "where did you get that voice, little girl?"

I smiled at my brother. "You are forgetting that I am not a little girl anymore. And the voice—a gift from God!"

"You will always be a little girl to me, Giovanna; I don't care how old you are!"

For a moment, I fell silent. "What is it Giovanna?"

"I was thinking of Papa," I said sadly. "What you just said is something he might have said to me."

Renzo took my hand, and we walked home in silence—each of us with our own memories of our father. In our hearts he remained alive and loved.

During the short time I was working for shoes, I was also spending time with my first cousin on my mother's side of the family, Jacobe. Almost from the first moment I had arrived in Tripoli, and we had become reacquainted, Jacobe seemed to always be around. He insisted on picking me up from Renzo's home and showing me the city as it had become after the war. For several weeks, Jacobe took me to dinner and theater, bought me gifts—even clothing. I was thankful to have such a wonderful and generous relative.

Unknowingly to me, Mustafa was also bidding for my time. He was an Arab friend from my childhood. As children, we had played together in his home next door to Aunt Misa. I was told that he had gone to London to the university for his education and had returned to Tripoli. When he learned that I too had returned to the city, he immediately sent word through my Aunt Misa that he would like to see me. Aunt Misa then relayed the message to my Aunt Regina, the self-proclaimed monarch of my mother's family. My mother's Aunt Regina then summoned me.

I had learned that Aunt Regina had become just short of a legend among our Jewish relatives. During the Holocaust, she and her husband and daughter had been taken prisoners by the Germans and sent to Auschwitz. She often recounted the horrors of the concentration camp, the cruelty they and the others had endured, and the numerous times she and her family had been marched to the "showers." Each time, as they were herded with the other prisoners, there was dread and uncertainty—they never knew if they were destined for the gas chambers. Amazingly, Aunt Regina, her husband, and their daughter had been spared. It was not until after the war that she was told they were allowed to live because her husband was British, and the family had British citizenship. They had been kept alive to be used as hostages should the need present itself.

I felt that Aunt Regina was about to tell me awful news—perhaps news about my mother. I didn't know. This "meeting" felt a lot like the ones I had with

Mother Superior at the convent in Arenella. I gave my aunt a kiss and waited for her to initiate the conversation.

"Have you news of your mother, Giovanna?"

I sighed in relief. "So this wasn't about my mother," I thought. "I have had no word from her since arriving in Tripoli, *Zia* (Aunt)." I answered.

"Ah," she responded as she nodded her head. Then from out of nowhere she asked, "What have you to say about Mustafa?"

I was puzzled. I could barely remember the little Arab boy and his siblings; I knew Jews and Arabs were no longer on friendly terms. "What do you mean *Zia?*"

"He wants to see you and has made it quite clear that he will not take 'no' for an answer. "Does he have some reason to see you Giovanna?"

I stared at my elderly white haired relative whose meeting seemed more like an interrogation. "I have not seen nor heard from Mustafa since we played as children. I have no idea what he wants!" It was difficult to keep the irritation out of my voice. "Why would Mustafa want to see me now?" I thought.

"Then you don't know?" she stated with some surprise.

"Know what?'

"Mustafa wants to marry you!"

29

A tremendous burden had been placed on my shoulders since my arrival in Tripoli. I already felt responsible for the welfare of my little brother, and now I was given the added worry that harm might come to him or me from Mustafa.

The relationship between the Jews and the Arabs had been deteriorating since the State of Israel began to rise in the late forties. Jewish people in North Africa as well as the Middle East and other Arab nations were facing prejudice and inequity. Arab uprising broke out against many Jewish communities. Pillaging and burning of Jewish synagogues, homes and shops became commonplace, and hundreds of Jews were murdered and imprisoned.

I felt safe with Jacobe. My Aunt Regina had warned me that Mustafa was capable of kidnapping me to make me his bride if he so chose. "Never go out alone," she said.

I heeded my aunt's warnings and was always accompanied by Jacobe, Renzo, or a friend during the following weeks, especially in the evenings. Perhaps I was just a naive young girl who had been through and seen so much during the war, that with the exception of Mustafa, I did not feel threatened in my own city. I was Italian! It never occurred to me that some might still think of me as Jewish.

My brother Renzo had become my protector. I was happy I had him and his family to watch over Guido and me. Although living in such tight quarters must have been difficult for Renzo and Pina, they were tolerant of the situation. Even so, I continued my search for a job and a home for my baby brother and me.

My first realization of the gravity of the situation between Jews and Arabs came one day as we were enjoying our noon meal at Pina's table. The blood-chilling screams were coming from somewhere outside and down below my brother's apartment. Renzo and I jumped up from the table and ran to the window—right behind us were Guido and Pina. From the third floor window of Renzo's apartment, we could not see the source of the screams. Pina picked up the baby, and without hesitation, we all ran out of the apartment and up the stairs to the rooftop. (In Tripoli, the roofs where flat and were used by the occupants of the apartment building for family gatherings, festivities, or just a place to sit and read.)

Renzo's apartment building was on a corner. From the rooftop, we were able to see for several blocks in all directions. The screams continued—loud agonizing screams. Some of the screams sounded like pleading. Then silence. Our eyes frantically searched the streets and apartments below us. Then I saw them. "There," I said, as I pointed to the Arabs carrying furniture and cloth sacks full of stolen goods from an apartment on the ground level of the building adjacent to ours. The men were going in and out of the apartment door much like a colony of ants; each returning with a treasure of some kind. There was no way to get an accurate count of their numbers or to recognize their faces.

"*Dio Mio,*" ("My God") cried Pina, "a Jewish family lives there!"

Renzo grabbed Pina's arm, then reached for me. "Get away from there Giovanna! They will see us!"

I slapped away his hand; I could not tear myself away from the sight before me! My first inclination was to run down to help the stricken family. I was torn with fear and guilt for not being able to do anything but watch! Then, at the next corner, I saw a British armored car approaching the scene. "Yes, yes!" I began waving my arms. "Help! Help!" I screamed.

Renzo had come back to the spot where I was standing and was ready to physically take me to safety when I began waving my arms. "What is it? What do you see?" demanded my frantic brother.

"There," I said as I pointed down the street. "Do you see it?"

When Renzo spotted the British vehicle, he too began to yell and wave his arms—we tried with all our might to get their attention. The car slowed to a stop. "They hear us!" I cried. I began screaming at the top of my lungs and pointing in the direction of the looting. "There! There! Help them! Please help them!"

The armored car approached the scene. Renzo grabbed me, ready again to keep me from being seen—neither of us could move! We stood frozen at the edge of the roof as we witnessed the armored car backing up and turning around. They had seen the mob of Arabs; there was no way they could not, and they chose not to get involved!

"Cowards!" I screamed and cried, "British cowards!" It was useless.

An entire Jewish family had been murdered, their possessions shared among the intruders. No one survived! No one was punished! It was the new Tripoli.

30

Only a few weeks after I had witnessed the atrocity in my neighborhood, a new Jewish girlfriend invited me to her home to meet her parents. Lydia was a very nice girl who was about my age. We seemed to have much in common. Her parents were much older than I had expected, and they lived in a modest little house in the city. For protection against the common crimes against their kind, the old couple kept a huge dog chained inside their home. *Cane Lupo* (Wolf Dog) began barking and growling at me as soon as he saw me. I wasn't afraid of the dog, but I didn't go near him. One could see the dog was very aggressive. He was trained to protect! To kill!

Lydia and her parents listened in amazement to my story of Italy and the war. Although they stayed in Tripoli during the time I had been sent away, they now wished they had gone to Israel. Because of their age, the couple no longer felt capable of enduring such a trip and the burden of beginning a new life in another country.

I envied Lydia for still having her parents to protect and love her. My father would have been about the same age as hers was now. "How ironic," I thought.

The entire visit was filled with the constant barking of the dog and the embarrassed apologies from its owners. I tried my best to ignore *Cane Lupo's* angry growls as I was saying my good-byes to Lydia and her parents. My back was turned towards the animal when suddenly, I felt the tremendous weight of the dog as he lunged against me, and the agonizing pain as his teeth pierced my calf. I fell to the marble floor and screamed in pain as I tried desperately to kick the dog off of me.

Lydia's father grabbed the broken chain and pulled the animal off of my leg before his huge jaws could bite down once again. A large pool of blood collected under me. I cried in pain. Lydia ran into the kitchen and grabbed a towel. Her mother used her teeth to rip a long piece of the cloth to wrap around my leg to stop the bleeding. They never stopped apologizing and praying while they rushed me to the nearby hospital.

The hospital staff must have thought I was another Jewish victim of the Arab persecution when they spoke to Lydia's parents. Before the elderly couple had a chance to say anymore, I told the nurses that I did not want Lydia or her parents to come into the treatment room with me. I had my reasons. The doctor asked me repeatedly about the dog. Did I know the dog? Could I describe the dog? Where could they find this dog? I knew the concern was that a rabid animal was loose in the streets of Tripoli. I lied. "I don't know the dog," I stated, "and I don't know where it lives." *Cane Lupo*, as dreadful as he was, remained the only protection Lydia's family had against the Arab threat—the only weapon they could afford. I could not find it in my heart to turn the animal in to the authorities to be killed. With no proof of whether or not I had been bitten by a sick animal, I was forced to undergo the treatment for rabies. Ten very painful injections in my stomach seemed a small price to pay for the lives of my Jewish friends.

For weeks I suffered with a festering wound to my calf. After an aggressive treatment of antibiotics, the wound finally healed. I never regretted or questioned my decision concerning the dog.

31

It came as a surprise when I received word that my Aunt Regina wanted to speak to me again. What more could be wrong? Was there more news about Mustafa? Had something horrible happened in our family? I had no idea why she wanted to see me again so soon!

After inquiring about my mother and brothers, Regina quite calmly came to the point of the visit. "When do you want to marry Jacobe?"

Had I been on the edge of a chair, I would have surely fallen off! "What?" I asked in complete surprise.

"Jacobe," she repeated. "When do you want to start the marriage preparations?"

"I don't understand," I replied. "I am not marrying Jacobe! He's my cousin!"

She must have been equally surprised at my outburst. "Giovanna," she said sternly, "it has come to my attention that your dear mother made a promise to her dying sister."

I was equally as stern. "What sister? What promise?" I asked in total bewilderment.

Aunt Regina stared at me for the longest time before answering. She was annoyed by my insolence. "You will watch your tone Giovanna!"

"I am sorry *Zia,* but I am totally baffled by what you are telling me.

"Your mother promised you to Jacobe. It was her oldest sister's dying wish that you and her son, your cousin, would be married one day. Now Jacobe has come to me and asked that I speak to you. It was a solemn vow made before God, Giovanna."

I just shook my head, "No, no, no, no!" I replied. "I will not, can not marry Jacobe!" There was no way I was going to marry my first cousin. My mother had never said anything about this promise to me! I excused myself and ran out of my aunt's house. "What is happening?" I thought as I ran down the street with tears streaming down my face. "First Mustafa, and now, Jacobe!" My mind suddenly took me back in time to Giulio. I began to sob without a care of who might see me!

The news was not well received by Jacobe. He must have waited his entire life for the promise between the two sisters to be fulfilled. To his misfortune, he had fallen in love with me during our time together. It pained me to hear what the news of my rejection had done to him, but I also knew I had done nothing to encourage any romantic inclinations he might have had towards me. The entire time I was with him, I thanked God for having such a wonderful and generous relative; I had no idea he thought he was courting his bride-to-be!

The brokenhearted Jacobe sold his electrical supply business and left Tripoli. He traveled to the city of Milano, Italy to await the next ship to Israel. I did not hear from him or of him again until months later when I received the news from my Aunt Regina that he had been killed in Italy. My Aunt Selma in Bologna had sent the newspaper article to her relatives in Tripoli. Jacobe had been killed by a mob of Italian men in a park in Milano. The Italians evidently thought the young Jewish man had molested a little Italian girl in the bushes in the park. After they had beaten him to death, the little girl admitted that the "nice gentle-man" was helping her find her ball which she lost in the shrubbery. Her tears were not from pain, but for her lost ball!

Aunt Regina read the article to me in such a way that I knew she and the rest of the relatives were blaming me for the ill fate of my cousin. "Had you only married him....," I heard over and over again. It was just one of many burdens of guilt I would carry for the rest of my life.

32

Although I loved the occasional singing at the cinema, it was not going to pay the rent. I had already earned my beautiful brown leather shoes by working in my cousin's shop, now I knew I had to continue to search for a real job. The quest for relatives with businesses was fruitless. So many of them had already left Tripoli or had lost their properties to the Arabs.

Jobs I was qualified for were practically non-existent. If only I had been able to finish my studies, I could have been teaching. There was no need for me to ponder over something I could not make happen at this point of my life.

While walking in the city one day, I happened upon a small photographer's studio with a "help wanted" sign in the window. I dared to hope the position was still available, or that it might be work I could do with my limited skills. Mr. LoBianco was the owner and also the photographer. "I am a hard worker sir," I said with a bright smile. "I learn very quickly too."

Mr. LoBianco didn't seem to be paying much attention to what I was saying.

Instead, he seemed to be studying my face. "I am sorry," he finally said, "what did you say?"

"I was saying…."

"Never mind," he interrupted, and for a moment my heart fell to my pretty brown leather clad feet. I thought for sure he was ending the interview.

"I need someone who can attend to the front counter and run the cash register while I am with my clients or working in the darkroom. Can you do that?"

It was hard for me to contain myself. "Yes, yes," I said, "I can do that. I worked at my cousin's shoe store and did those very things!" I knew I had not worked for shoes for nothing!

"Can you speak English?" He asked almost as an afterthought.

Immediately I smiled and thought, "Thank you *Madrina*," as I introduced myself to my prospective employer in English, and acting as if he were a client I said, "How may I help you sir?"

He was impressed with my knowledge of the English language, apparently he had English speaking customers as well as the locals. I was hired.

Only days after I began working at the photography studio, Mr. LoBianco insisted that I allow him to take my photograph. At first I was a little leery. "What kind of photos are you speaking of?" I asked.

He grinned as if he knew what I might be thinking. "Just your face, little one! Just your beautiful face!"

After much discussion, I finally agreed. Even though I had insisted he put someone else's photograph in its place, the finished image was placed on display in the front window of his shop. "This is my studio," he reminded me.

The English captain came into the studio to have film developed. He immediately recognized me as being the girl in the photograph in the window. "That's quite a lovely photo of you in the window," he commented. "Very beau-ti-ful!" He spoke slowly and circled his face with his index finger.

I smiled. I knew he thought I didn't speak his language and was carefully enunciating each word. "Thank you," I said shyly, "Mr. LoBianco is very good at what he does; he made me look much better than I really do!" Although my English was not very good, the young Englishman seemed very surprised and pleased. I was honest in my remark; I still maintained the teachings of the nuns about vanity.

"I think you are quite beautiful," he replied, "quite the model actually." He smiled. He was attractive in a boyish sort of way. His blue eyes and curly blond hair were certainly indicative of his English heritage. Even that first day, he took his time in the shop, looking at the photographs on the walls, and occasionally glancing over at me. He acted as though he had no where else to go.

After that first meeting, Samuel Walker found any excuse to come into the shop. He brought in more film to be developed than any of the other customers, and each time he found some excuse to remain in the shop. "It must be fascinating to be able to take such good pictures," he would say. "I am just a beginner really…you can probably tell by the number of photos I take."

"Yes," I said in amusement, "you do use a lot of film."

"Well then, I guess I'll be going." He backed out of the front door. "Later then?"

"Goodbye Mr. Walker."

"Call me Samuel if you like."

I smiled. "Alright. Goodbye Mr. Samuel Walker."

He nodded his head and grinned. "Cheerio."

"Ciao."

This casual flirtation continued for a few days. Finally, one afternoon he offered to walk me home. During one of our previous conversations, I had mentioned to him how frightened I was of walking in that part of town alone. In the back of my mind, I still feared that Mustafa might appear one evening and take me.

Unconsciously I had given Samuel Walker a perfect reason to spend time with me outside of the photography studio.

Samuel was very much the gentleman and a wonderful conversationalist. We walked down the streets of Tripoli talking and laughing at some funny story he would tell me about his friends. When we arrived at Renzo's apartment building, Samuel turned to face me. For a moment I did not know what to do or think. He picked up my right hand and kissed it. It was a brief kiss—but a kiss nonetheless. I was quite surprised and embarrassed. Nothing even remotely similar had happen since the brief kiss on my lips from Friar Melchizedek in Florence. "Could we go out sometime?" he asked.

Still stunned and a bit puzzled at what had just happened, I managed to squeak out a timid, "Okay!"

Samuel grinned. "Jolly good!"

Renzo and Pina were very pleased with Samuel. He was friendly and polite, with noticeably good breeding, and he seemed quite taken with me. Even though the extent of our intimacy was still a kiss on my hand, after only a few months of friendship, he asked me to marry him. "Why not?" I thought. Again I replied with my favorite English word, "Okay!"

As we waited for Samuel's mother to send the heirloom engagement ring from London, he and his friends threw a huge engagement party for us. Samuel played the piano; we all sang and danced and had a "jolly good time", as Samuel was fond of saying.

As I danced with my handsome brother Renzo, who was now taking the place of my beloved father during this happy occasion, he looked at me as if he were seeing me for the first time. "Do you love him Giovanna?" he asked with noticeable concern in his tone.

I smiled, or maybe I forced a smile, "I like him a lot," I said without hesitation. "He's a jolly good fellow!" By the look on my brother's face, I don't think it was the answer he was hoping for.

33

Just weeks after the engagement party, Samuel received orders to go to the Suez Canal. He was highly upset with the timing of his new assignment. "I don't want to leave you," he said over and over.

"Oh Samuel, it is only for a few months. I am not going anywhere," I assured him. His leaving did not seem to bother me as it should have. "It will be a good test of your love for me," I added.

"But I don't need to be tested. I do love you. You will wait for me—won't you?"

I rolled my eyes, "Silly English boy, yes, I will wait for you."

Lydia and her parents had not met Samuel, and I had promised them that I would bring my fiancé to meet them before he left. Samuel was always excited about meeting my friends or family. Perhaps he thought this simple gesture was proof of my love for him.

I was a little nervous about their dog, but I was determined not to make my friends uncomfortable with the memory of what had happened during my last visit. Samuel put a protective arm around my shoulder as we neared the house. To my relief, *Cane Lupo* had been locked in a utility room during our visit. Samuel held my hand; he could see that the barking and growling of the dog behind the closed door was affecting me.

After a short visit, I made some excuse to leave. I kept my eyes on the entrance to the utility room as I hurriedly made my way towards the front door. The dog, sensing my proximity, was now feverishly pounding his head against the door that separated him from me. Then to my horror, the huge animal broke through the wooden barrier, oblivious to the splintering wood as he charged straight for me. I only had time to gasp before I felt his huge muscular body crash against me. The force of his attack knocked me to the ground. I was eye to eye with the growling beast—his hot breath in my face! I couldn't breathe from the weight of him on top of me and from pure fear! I was certain that *Cane Lupo* was about to rip out my throat! I closed my eyes, unable to move, unable to scream! Then, just as suddenly as the animal had pinned me down, I felt him being pulled off of me. Samuel had grabbed the dog around the neck; he had risked his own life to save me!

I left my friend's home in tears, and I felt horrible about the worry and embarrassment I had put Lydia and her parents through once again. They kept apologizing as they cried with me. "What can we do? What can we do?" They kept saying.

"Nothing," I assured them. "He is a very good watch dog! You need him to protect you. I am fine—really."

In realty, I was in a state of shock and was oblivious to anyone or anything around me as Samuel kept my trembling body from collapsing on the sidewalk. I never knew what happened to the dog, if anything, but I never returned to Lydia's home again. I felt sorry for the old couple and almost felt responsible for the actions of their dog. He was doing what he was trained to do!

After that incident, Samuel became even more attentive and protective of me. He was reluctant to leave me, but his duty required that he go to the Suez Canal. As soon as he arrived at his new destination, he called to ask me if I would marry him by proxy. Laughingly, I told him he was being foolish, and that we would be married when he returned to Tripoli. Meanwhile, I assured him that I would be safe and would certainly avoid big dogs; and mostly likely, little dogs as well. I tried to ease his fears by telling him I would stay busy with my work and my family.

Although I was grateful for the job at the photographer's shop, it paid very little—not enough for me to afford my own apartment. I continued searching the newspaper ads until I found a position being advertised with the British airlines. It required an English speaking individual to greet and assist arriving airline passengers. I was hired right away.

The airport was a substantial distance outside of Tripoli, but I was excited to have been hired as a ground hostess. Once again, I felt thankful to my godmother who had insisted I learn the English language. Unfortunately, the only available shift was at night, and it was a struggle for me to stay awake.

"Ladies and gentlemen, welcome to Tripoli, Libya. Those passengers who have come to their destination, please proceed to the customs building. For those of you who have connecting flights, please follow me." My speech to the passengers was rehearsed and brief, peppered in with a few questions from the passengers. It was not as glamorous a job as I had originally thought, but it paid well.

Night after night, I boarded the planes. Most of the time everything went smoothly; the passengers did as they were instructed. Other times, I wondered how long I could maintain the facade.

"Excuse me, Miss." The very well dressed English woman had flagged me down from her seat. "Are those Eucalyptus trees I saw at the end of the runway?"

I stared at her, trying to understand what it was she had just asked me. I was not familiar with the word "Eucalyptus" and thought she was just pronouncing a familiar word in an unfamiliar way!

"Eucalyptus?" I repeated.

"Tree, tree girl! Don't you speak English?" She was arrogant and nasty and upset me to the point of tears.

34

Every attempt to make the night shift easier on my body failed. I was a creature of habit. All those years of early morning Mass and early bedtime hours were still a part of my body's clock. The long bus ride out to the airport also added to my misery.

The advertisement for the opening at a coffee shop in the city near the cinema house caught my attention. With a little luck, the pay would be good enough for me to quit my hostess position. The European coffee shops were a favorite meeting place for both young and old. They served everything from coffee, beer, and sandwiches, to ice cream. The thought of working in that type of surrounding was appealing to me, and something I would enjoy. Having young people, happy people around me, would be a refreshing change.

I sat alone at a small table inside coffee shop while I waited for the owner to return. Minutes later, four young American soldiers entered the shop and immediately spotted me sitting alone. "Well, hello there *signorina*," one of them said as they walked straight to my table. "What's your name darlin'?"

I pretended not to hear them. "Ah, come on darlin'...."

"No speak English!" I lied as I turned my back to them.

They circled the table like wolves. One of them sat down across from me and continued asking my name while the others laughed and made jokes.

"Ya'll leave her alone!" The young American soldier who spoke was tall and slender with dark hair and hazel eyes. He approached the table and greeted the others. Apparently he had come to the coffee shop to meet his friends.

"Ah Smitty," one of them said, "we ain't harmin' the gal none!"

The one they called "Smitty" didn't smile, "I said, ya'll leave her alone!" He stepped over to the one seated across from me and put a firm hand on his shoulder. "There's a table over yonder Billy. Why don't ya'll go over there?"

Billy got up without an argument, "Want her all to yourself, don't cha Smitty?" He mumbled under his breath as he and his buddies walked away. Whatever conversation they were having must have been amusing. Their laughter was unnerving. I rose from my seat.

"No need to leave miss," said the one they had called "Smitty". The tall American looked at me; he seemed genuinely embarrassed, "I'm sorry, Miss," he said.

I sat back down. "Thank you very much," I answered. I wasn't aware of it, but I must have been smiling at him.

He smiled back. "So, you do speak English!"

I got up from the table once again. I was convinced that this new fellow would now take his turn to embarrass me. "Only a little," I said, this time without a smile. "I am sorry; I must leave now." I made my way past him, avoiding eye contact with him and his friends. If this was what I had to face each day in this shop, then maybe it wasn't something I was ready to do. Perhaps the fact that the owner had not returned to interview me was a sign. I left the coffee shop without the thought of ever returning again unescorted.

Giovanna
1947

35

I was hesitant to apply for a job at Wheelus Field, the American military base. My feelings about the Americans had changed very little since I had left Florence, but I was desperate for work. Ironically, I was hired to work the cash register at the snack bar that was next to the base's airfield.

The snack bar was always full of hungry young soldiers—both male and female. The lunch hour was especially hectic. The strong odor of the fried potatoes the Americans called "French fries," and the "hamburgers," was going to take me a while to get accustomed to. I thought it unusual that these Americans liked foods with foreign names or words. Then there was their "hot dog" which I was told by other Italians was much like a tasteless sausage.

Although I was very nervous at first, I was happy to have found a job so close to home and with a good salary. I was able to run the cash register without too much trouble, although sometimes it was difficult for me to figure out how much American change was due back after a sale.

Everyone that came through the line to pay for their food was considerate and patient. I had come to the conclusion that Americans were not such a bad lot. The young Americans seemed to enjoy life as much as any Italian youths. Sometimes men tried to initiate a conversation with me while I was working, but I simply said, "I am to be married—thank you—goodbye." And they would move on.

Sometimes I would think about all those years I had studied in hopes of becoming an educator; all those dreams of the university seemed so far away and impossible now. I was nineteen-years-old and still living with my half-brother and sister-in-law; I was desperately trying to earn enough money to provide for my brother Guido and myself, and I was engaged to an English soldier who I barely knew.

My mind must have been a thousand miles away when the young airman spoke.

"You owe me a dime, Miss!" I looked up to see the smiling face of the young man who had come to my rescue in the coffee shop in the city. It had been several weeks since that day, and I had all but forgotten about him. He was smiling at me with his hand outstretched. He was more handsome than I remembered.

"Oh, I am so sorry!" I said as I handed him his change. "You are the boy from the coffee shop—yes?"

He put the dime in his pocket. "Well, I don't think I'm a boy, but yeah, I'm that fella. My name is Ford Smith; what's your name?"

I knew that his friends had called him "Smitty", and I did not connect "Smitty" with the name Smith. In all my studies of the English language, the name "Smith" was associated with many of the fictional characters in the stories I had read. I thought he was lying to me about his name. "I am sorry," I said, as I pointed to the growing line of people waiting to check out.

Reluctantly, he proceeded to his table. I couldn't help glancing up at him from time to time, and each time I did, he was staring at me with a smile on his face. I recognized one of his buddies as he came through the check out, and he recognized me. Without hesitation I interrupted his attempts at flirtation and boldly asked him the name of the GI that had helped me in the city. His shoulders fell, "You mean Smitty?"

"Yes, I know you called him 'Smitty'," I said. "Does he have another name?"

"Yeah, Ford Smith," he replied downheartedly, "an Alabama boy I think."

I smiled and thanked him as I handed him his change. "Ford Smith," I thought, "the name of an American automobile—how peculiar." I glanced up again at Smitty; he was gone.

Ford Smith
1947

36

Ford Smith came into the snack bar every day, sometimes twice a day. From his uniform, the patches on his sleeves, and the pistols on his hips I knew he was in the Military Police, "MP's" as they were called. Whenever he or any other MP walked in, there seemed to be a lot less commotion in the snack bar. That demand for respect was rather appealing to me.

Smitty would always buy something when he came to the snack bar. He would slide his tray with his hamburger or hotdog, his French fries, and his soda in front of me, and nonchalantly say "hello" as he checked out. I, in turn, would thank him, then look to the next person in line. It never failed to amuse me—Smitty would find himself a table where he could position his chair in order to see me. Occasionally I would glance up at him, and he would pretend to look away.

Finally one day, while he was waiting for his change, he calmly asked, "Would you like to go for a walk with me when you get off?"

The sudden question from the man who had pretended to ignore me for the past several days came as a complete surprise. I didn't know what to say at first. "What harm could a walk with him do," I rationalized. I at least owed him that much for being so kind to me in the city. "Do you mean today?" I asked as I thought things through.

"Yeah, I was thinkin' today."

"Okay!" I replied. "But please, no pistols."

He smiled and nodded his head. "Well okay then! No, *problema,* I'll leave them behind," he said, the excitement evident in his voice.

We met just inside the base airport terminal. Although he was right on time, he seemed rushed and had not yet taken off his pistols. When he saw me looking at the guns, he apologized. "I got caught up in somethin'," he explained. "Is it still alright?"

"Sure—okay," I nodded. I felt a little foolish that I had even made such a request. I motioned towards the ladies room. "I will be back. I must wash my hands. Okay?" I couldn't possibly tell him I needed to use the toilet; I would have rather died than mention the word! Again, the life in the convent was to blame.

He nodded, "I'll be right over yonder."

I knew he was watching me walk away from him, and I felt very self-conscious. Finally I turned the corner and was out of his sight. Just as I reached the restroom door, another GI approached me. He was also very handsome, and I recognized him as being one of the men Smitty would sit with in the snack bar sometimes. "Listen, beautiful," he said, "you shouldn't go out with that guy—he's engaged you know! What you need is a real man. You should go out with me—Johnny!" With that statement, he lifted me off my feet and kissed me on my mouth. My hands flew up to his chest, and I pushed him away with all my strength. As soon as my feet hit the ground, I ran into the bathroom, out of breath and totally bewildered!

Smitty had not witnessed any of the exchange between his friend and me. He had been waiting patiently as he had said he would. He saw me walking toward him and must have noticed the irritation on my face. "Somethin' wrong?" he asked.

When I told him what had happened, he became enraged. With his hands on his pistols he said rather calmly, "Johnny huh, I'll take care of him! You wait for me!"

He left me standing there in the middle of the terminal and headed straight for the barracks to find his friend. My initial thoughts of leaving were not as strong as my curiosity about these Americans. I waited.

Smitty returned a short time later. He was strangely calm and was no longer wearing his pistols. I had no idea what had transpired between the two men, and I was afraid to ask. There were no signs on Smitty that would indicate he had been in a fight; I just hoped he had not shot his friend! "Nah, I didn't kill him," he reassured me as he saw my concern. "He ran like a yella bellied coward. He ain't worth me goin' to jail—that's for sure. But I ain't done with that boy yet, and he knows it." Smitty was grinning.

We walked for a short distance around the base. I asked him about his fiancé. "How'd you know about that?" he asked, and then stopped himself. "Johnny?"

"*Si,*" I said, "it was your friend."

"Well that….! Yeah, I was engaged—I mean I am, but I can't marry that girl. I don't love her. Don't get me wrong—she's nice, but she's German, and she loves Hitler. That's just un-American! What about you? I hear you're supposed to marry some English fella."

"Oh," I said with surprise. I didn't remember telling him I was engaged either.

"Yes," I admitted, "his name is Samuel. He is in the Suez now, but when he returns, we will get married. He will be back soon—I think!"

Smitty stopped for a moment. "How soon?" he asked.

"Oh, I don't actually know. He just tells me 'soon'."

Smitty seemed relieved—as if my answer had given him hope. So, from that evening on, we would take a walk after I got off from work. I think we must have been a strange sight from the very beginning—a six-foot American soldier and a four-foot, ten-inch Italian girl. We walked very closely, side by side, but never touching. He was in fact allowing me come to my own conclusions about my relationship with Samuel.

37

A few days after the incident at the terminal, Johnny came to the snack bar. He had chosen to eat his lunch much earlier in the day than usual. My guess was that he was trying to avoid bumping into Smitty. As he was paying for his meal, his attempts at flirtation were met with no encouragement from me. I was still feeling quite odd and embarrassed about what he had done.

"Well hello again," he said brightly as if he was surprised to have bumped into me at the snack bar. "Would you like to go out to a show sometime?"

"Here is your change," I said coolly. "Cheerio!"

"Cheerio? What the…ohhh, that's right; you're engaged to some British fella."

Suddenly, someone came up behind Johnny and grabbed him by his collar.

The tray full of food went crashing to the floor as the surprised airman spun around. "Hey, Smitty…Ford, let go man!" Johnny seemed genuinely nervous.

Ford was in his uniform with his pistols worn securely on his hips. He held on to Johnny's collar as he dragged him out of the line. "If you ever touch that girl again, I swear I'll kill ya." He spoke softly and calmly, but there was no mistaking the dangerous tone of his voice.

"Sure son, I was only playing! You know me Ford!" Johnny quickly stepped away from Smitty, straightened his shirt, then turned and hurried out the door.

"Why did you do that?" I asked. The scene had caused quite a stir among the other soldiers in the room. I felt as though everyone where laughing and talking about me. I looked around the room. Everyone seemed to be waiting for my reaction and subsequent discussion with the man who had come to my rescue. It annoyed me even more that these Americans were enjoying this little drama at my expense. "You must think I am unable to take care of myself. You are mistaken you know. I am quite capable, and I can speak to whomever I please!" I wondered who I was trying to convince.

There were a few chuckles in the room. Ford turned around to stare at the source—the chuckles stopped abruptly. He smiled, not seeming to hear my last statement, as if he knew a secret that I wasn't aware of. "After work then," he stated with confidence.

I was strangely excited about meeting him for our walk. Emotions stirred within me that were unfamiliar. I couldn't recall a time when I had been so anxious, yet so eager to be with anyone—including Samuel. There was no way I would allow myself to show this handsome American how he made me feel. I thought I hid my feelings of excitement rather well.

As I rushed out of the snack bar, I nearly ripped my apron off my waist, then stuffed it in my bag. Smitty was already waiting for me in the same spot where we had met the day before.

I again pointed to the restroom. "Just give me a moment," I said.

"I know," he interrupted, "you want to wash your hands." He was smiling as if he knew my excuse was a phony. "I think I'll walk you over there this time."

"No, no, I can go alone. It will be alright."

"I need to wash my hands too, and I'll be right next door if you need me."

I just didn't know what to say to this man. I was never accompanied to the toilet by a man! It was just never done! As horrified as I was, I had no choice but to let him do whatever he wanted to do.

I apologized for smelling so much like the snack bar. Guido had often remarked that I smelled like the American hamburger and fried potatoes when I came home from work. Smitty just smiled at my concern. "I like hamburgers," he said.

Our walks around the base finally led to walks around the city, but only in the evenings when the streets were more deserted. I knew better than to be seen with a Yankee boy in broad daylight. Many Italians were not fond of the Americans. An Italian girl seen with one was automatically branded a whore!

Occasionally I would get a call from Samuel, but Ford, if he were there during the call, would whisper to me to tell the English boy to stop bothering me. "Stop," I commanded him, "he is my fiancé!" I knew that I could not marry Samuel. I did not love him; I also felt that it would be too cruel to tell him about Ford over the telephone. Samuel had been too kind to me, and the memories of my rejection of Jacobe were still fresh in my mind.

When Samuel returned, I was honest with him about spending time with the American soldier. I tried to explain how we met by accident, that Ford had protected me from bullies. "It had never been my intention to continue seeing him, it just happened!" I explained to the very worried Englishman.

"Darling Giovanna, what are you telling me? You promised to marry me when I returned! I know you love me—do you not?"

Nothing I could say made it easier for me to break off the engagement.

"Samuel," my voice quivered, "you are a very nice man, a wonderful man! I...I just do not love you. I am very sorry."

Samuel did not accept what was happening. To him, I had been a victim of harassment from the American soldier. He must have thought that somehow I had been persuaded or forced into seeing Smitty; surely his sweet Italian girl would never have gone on her own accord! "No, no, no! You don't mean it! I know you don't mean it. Look," he said as he pulled a small box out of his pocket, "it's my grandmama's wedding ring—your ring now!"

I gasped when I saw the beautiful diamond ring. Then I looked up at Samuel; my heart went out to him. He just was not what I wanted.

Samuel refused to let me go. He went to his commander. Days later, Ford was called into the office of his base commander. He was reprimanded for spending time with another man's fiancé and ordered not to see me again. He was threatened with reassignment and told that I would be banned from the base! I would lose my job.

My sister-in-law was infuriated when she learned I was seeing an American and had broken my engagement with Samuel. With her hands on her hips, she paced the floor in front of me. "How could you do such a thing? You are engaged to a wonderful boy! A very rich boy! You have lost your mind! You <u>will</u> marry him, Giovanna!"

"I don't love him!" I screamed back. "No Pina, I will not marry Samuel just because you like him! You marry him!" The slap across my face came as a shock and brought pain to my very soul. "I must leave here," I said calmly as I felt the tears in my eyes. I knew that if my brother Renzo found out his wife had struck his little sister, all hell would pay!

When I approached my brother Renzo, he immediately knew something was wrong. "What is it Giovanna?"

I began crying once again, but this time it was not from the slap; I was afraid I was going to disappoint my brother with my decision about Samuel. "I broke off my engagement to Samuel, Renzo. I am so sorry!"

"Why are you apologizing to me?" He asked as he held out his arms. "This is your decision and yours alone."

"I don't love him Renzo," I explained as he held me in his arms.

"I know," he answered. "I know."

38

Even though Renzo protested my leaving his home, I thanked him and Pina for letting us stay with them. It was time for Guido and me to find a place of our own. We moved into an apartment with another Italian girl I had met at work. It was the only thing I could afford to do. This arrangement only lasted a short time—the social life of my friend, a single young woman, was not conducive to raising my little brother. I needed something more stable for Guido.

The middle-aged Jewish couple welcomed my brother and me into their home. I had learned that they had a room to rent and had gone to inquire. There was an immediate feeling of comfort and safety within their walls. Nino and Rubina were childless and full of love to give to us from the moment we met. There was no question in my mind that this would be the perfect home for us, but I had no idea at that time that this couple would become among the most loved people in my life!

Nino and Rubina

It was the perfect solution for my brother and me—we had the parent figures we so needed in our lives, and Rubina's live-in nephew became the perfect playmate for Guido. They also had no objections to the American boy, and in fact, they became quite fond of "Smith". I could tell from the very beginning that this American was not accustomed to the outward demonstration of affection that was given so freely by Rubina and Nino. Although reluctant at first, he soon began to appreciate the nurturing bestowed upon us by this wonderful Jewish couple.

Ford and Guido 1948

Despite the warnings of the base commander, Smitty and I continued to meet each day after work. I imagine the word had gotten out that we had broken our former marriage engagements, and we were in fact free to see each other. Nevertheless, we were careful about who saw us together.

Our new meeting place on our days off from work was a secluded area on the beach within the base perimeter. We both had an affinity for the sun and the sea.

At first I refused to purchase a swimsuit and would sit on the sand and watch as Smitty plunged head on into the inviting waters of the Mediterranean.

Smitty had chosen the spot and dubbed it "Smitty's Beach!" He worked endless hours building a makeshift tent from fallen palm leaves he had gathered from the shoreline. After we consumed our picnic lunch of bread and cheese, and a bottle of red wine, we would lay side-by-side on a rough military issued blanket and fall asleep.

I loved the way he smelled, clean like soap. I took in big breaths of him as I nestled my head on his shoulder—it felt like a safe place, like home. We were impervious to the heat of the North African sun. More than once we awoke with an audience of airmen watching and teasing us from the shore.

"The water is warm; you really need to get yourself a swimsuit," he said one day as he emerged from the water.

I watched him as he approached the blanket and shook his wet hair all over me. "Ah," I screamed in delight, "you are a crazy American, Smitty!"

He sat down on the blanket beside me, and then leaned back on his elbows.

"You know…you can call me Ford if you like. 'Smitty', well that's just a nickname the guys use."

He pulled me down on top of him. "Okay, okay," I began to laugh, "Faurrd." Apparently I was rolling my r's.

"Fo-rd," he said slowly.

"Ah, idiota," ("idiot") I teased him, "Ford!"

"Well, that's better," he said as he kissed me. His lips set my entire body on fire, and for a moment I forgot everything I had ever learned in church. Ford rolled me over on the blanket, and I felt the weight of his wet body.

"No, no, no," I said as I pushed him off. "You mustn't!"

The disappointed young man immediately released me. "I'm sorry honey," he said, "I just can't help it. You are just so beautiful."

After a few embarrassing moments, we dragged our blanket under the palm leaves of our makeshift tent to make use of the little shade it rendered. Ford opened the bottle of wine while I prepared our food.

"Tell me about your home in America. Is it very nice?" I asked.

Ford began to laugh. "Nice? It's a farm. Do you know what a farm is?"

"Ma si!" ("Yes, of course!") I answered with a little irritation at such a stupid question. "You remember that I studied English?"

"Sorry. Well, I lived on a farm in Brent, Alabama."

"Where is this Brent?"

"Nowhere really," he said, "just a small town—probably on nobody's map!"

"You had cows then?"

Ford seemed excited over my curiosity about America and his home in Alabama. "Yes—cows, pigs, chickens, mules...regular farm. My daddy raised cotton. I was out in the fields when the sun came up, and didn't get back in until the sun went down."

"You did this by yourself?" I could only imagine what I had never seen.

"Naw, my brothers too, and the Negro farmhands we hired."

I watched him as he told me of his life on the farm. Sometimes he would laugh at some picture he had in his mind of his childhood. Other times, his face changed as a painful memory emerged.

I wanted to know everything about him. Although his background, education, and upbringing were so totally different than my own, I found his stories fascinating. There had been ten children born to his parents; he was somewhere in the middle of the birth order. Hard work and sweat had taken the place of his education past the seventh grade, but there was nothing ignorant about him. "Pop needed me in the cotton fields," he explained. "There just wasn't much need for schoolin' on a farm." He laughed as he recalled the hundreds of hot Alabama days he plowed the fields behind an old mule. He had lied about his age and joined the service at seventeen. "I couldn't wait to join up with Uncle Sam—I had to get away from that fartin' mule!" When he realized what he had said, he apologized profusely. He had forgotten about my Catholic upbringing, and that I never talked about bodily functions—mules' or human.

"What does it mean 'fartin'?" I asked quite innocently. When he explained, I was mortified, then seconds later I burst into laughter!"

His stories about his family: the playful episodes with his brothers that sometimes led to harsh consequences from his father, huge "home-style" meals, and working side by side with the Negro farm hands seemed almost romantic. I envied his memories of his family. The war had robbed me of time with my own family.

The Smith home in Brent, Alabama.

Ford Smith on the farm.
1938

Although in the beginning, I was too shy to put on a swimsuit, the heat and the enticing warm sea were too much to bear. To Ford's excitement, I entered one of the cabanas on the beach to change into my new swimsuit. The group of sailors must have been watching us. When they saw me go to the cabana, and Ford still on the blanket by the shore, they came up to the cabana and tried to peek through a small hole in the door. In an instance, Ford was at the cabana. He kicked his foot up, flicking sand into the faces of the sailors, then placed his foot squarely on the hole.

The sailors were angry. "Hey! What do you think you're doing? Get your big-ass foot off! You're outnumbered soldier!" they reminded him. "We could easily take your big foot off that door for you!"

"Ya'll have to kill me first," I heard him say without hesitation. Ford was angry. His foot never budged.

I held my breath, not knowing if in the next few moments the sailors would attack Ford and leave me helpless. To my relief, I heard the grumbling of the sailors as they went on about their business. "You alright in there Giovanna?" Ford had remained by my door.

"Yes, yes, I am okay. Did they hurt you?"

"Naw."

I could tell he was still outside the cabana. "What are you doing?" I checked the hole to make sure he wasn't looking in. I could see the back of his leg as he stood guard over me.

"You ever comin' out?" He finally asked.

I was frozen with fear. I had never put on a swimsuit and certainly had never been that exposed to a man before. "You go away," I ordered. "Go to the blanket! I am not ready yet!"

He did as he was told, but never took his eyes off of the cabana. Finally, I gathered enough courage to open the door and peek outside. I saw him watching me. *"Santa Maria!"* I whispered as I walked unto the hot sand. I could tell by the huge grin on his face that Ford liked what he saw!

Ford and Giovanna 1948

As I lay on the blanket, I could feel the warmth of the sand under my body as it penetrated through the blanket beneath me. I felt a sense of peace and contentment as I breathed in the salty aroma of the sea. I watched as the tall, bronzed American slowly walked into the emerald water. He turned and waved to me; his hazel eyes had taken on the color of the sea. "Come on in!" he beckoned as he slid down below the waves. He swam like a fish back to the surface. "The water is mighty fine!" he assured me as he brushed his wet hair from his face.

I smiled, and for the first time I knew what he had known from the start. I had met my destiny. Slowly, I got off the blanket and walked towards him. He never took his eyes off of me, not even for a moment. I walked straight into his arms; the arms that would hold me for the rest of my life.

Epilogue

Music and laughter filled the beautifully decorated room. Small groups of Italian women, all dressed for the happy occasion, shared some bit of news or gossip in their native tongue. Other friends and family gathered around the refreshment tables while they enjoyed the finger-foods and drinks. Except for the small children who amused themselves by climbing over and under the chairs, everyone was watching and listening to the men and women taking turns singing at the microphone.

A small television set sat on a table in the front of the room next to the white lace-draped table that proudly displayed the three-tiered cake. Through the large glass picture window, the Gulf of Mexico formed a beautiful backdrop for the celebration. There was a constant flow of images on the television screen—all in black and white photography. Each frame was of a person or an event that somehow seemed to have meaning enough to be captured on film.

Giovanna looked at her white-haired husband of fifty years, then at their six grown children. Their five sons had traveled down from their homes in the Atlanta area; a few had come alone, and the others had brought their families.

Their daughter, the oldest child, lived on the Mississippi Gulf Coast where she and her husband and three daughters had made their home. It was comforting for Giovanna and Ford to have her near them. It was evident as they watched their six children, that their daughter was still "in charge" of her brothers. It was she who had organized this celebration and had given each brother instructions as to how he was to do his part. The boys listened to their big sister—they always had.

Giovanna walked over to her husband and took his hand. He looked down at his tiny "Italian doll" and smiled. "They're somethin' aren't they?" he said as his wife dropped his hand and wrapped herself around one of his arms.

"Yes," she had to admit, "they are really something."

Had it all been worth it? Sometimes she wondered about the life she might have had if she had not met Ford. She remembered the day she left the American ship that was docked in the Port of Naples. After the young sailor had made such a fuss over her, she remembered thinking she could never become a nun. It was that day that she had decided what it was she wanted from her life: "A family. To sing. To teach." She thought about those ideals. Yes, she had been asked to sing with the USO in Tripoli, but her new husband would not allow it. In more recent years, she had taught the Italian language informally to people in the area who were about to visit Italy. It was a far cry from the university teaching position she had once hoped for. But family, "Oh yes," she thought, "I had my family!"

Because Ford had been underage, he needed his parents' permission to marry Giovanna. They had already given him their permission to marry his German fiancé, now he wanted to marry an Italian girl from North Africa. They were certain that their very southern son had been in the desert heat too long and had lost his mind! Anyone from North Africa had to be of the black race!

Ford would not let anything stand in his way; he would make Giovanna his wife no matter what he had to do! Finally, on May 7, 1949, the determined young soldier married the love of his life.

After her daughter was born, Giovanna and Ford had four sons—delivered nearly eighteen months apart. By the time Giovanna had reached her twenty-sixth birthday, she had given birth to five children. Five years later, they were surprised with yet another son. Only two of the six children were born in America; the others were born in Tripoli during two different tours of duty.

Giovanna wondered how she made it this far. The young wife and mother had found her life overwhelming. Less than two years after their marriage, tuberculosis finally claimed the life of her mother. She had never left the hospital in Naples. Giovanna, Ford, and their baby daughter had only one chance to visit Camilla before her death.

Guido was never allowed to accompany his sister to America. He had acquired tuberculosis himself and was hospitalized for an entire year before the Air Force would allow him to join Giovanna and her family in Aviano, Italy in 1958. Giovanna's beloved *Guiduccio* died of cancer in 1998 at the age of sixty-one.

Ford and Giovanna's life together was full of ups and downs. The intense and passionate love they had for one another was overshadowed by the immense burdens brought upon them by military life, children, sickness, emotional, and monetary problems. A malignant tumor was discovered on their third child's leg when he was only six weeks old. The overdose of radiation given to their baby left the young couple with years of worry, and a crippled son. Nearly every year after his birth, their son had to undergo orthopedic surgery to correct the ongoing bone growth abnormalities.

Many times the marriage teetered on the edge of destruction. But, it survived. It survived in part because Giovanna believed in family—the one dream she and

Ford had made come true. It survived because of Ford's strong will. It survived because that is what God had intended.

Giovanna looked around the room at her friends and family. "Who would have ever dreamed that my life would be here on the Mississippi Gulf Coast? No," she thought, "life has not turned out exactly how I had imagined." She would never live in the opulence she had known as a small child; she had long since come to terms with that fact. Instead, she treasured their small home in Biloxi where they had lived since 1968 after Ford retired from the Air Force.

Her children and some of her grandchildren were gathering at the microphone. Each of them took turns recounting some amusing story about the family's past, and telling tales on each other.

"I could have never hoped for a more wonderful family," Giovanna admitted to herself. Through the two of them, Ford and Giovanna had already given the world an exceptional singer and teacher, a nurse, a writer, a sculptor, several painters and photographers, and blossoming scholars. Best of all, the future held promise for their seventeen grand and great grandchildren who had yet to make their mark on the world.

The small television set continued to flash the images on its screen. Each photograph had been taken by Ford; each photograph had been composed with the artistic eye of a loving father and husband. He never imagined that one day the images would be strung together, almost like a movie, and be enjoyed by so many people.

Ford looked down at his beautiful wife. Yes, she had aged from time and circumstance, yet her hair showed no sign of graying. It was only her eyes that held a hint of sadness from the hardships she had endured for nearly all her life.

Ford didn't see any of those things. Instead, he still envisioned the pretty young Italian girl in the café in downtown Tripoli; he saw that exciting woman lying on the blanket on "Smitty's beach."

He stooped down and kissed her on the lips. "I love you honey."

Giovanna smiled as her face lifted up towards his. "I love you too."

The End

Giovanna and Ford Smith
Wedding Day ~ May 7, 1949

Ford and Giovanna Smith and Children
50th Wedding Anniversary
1999

Back from left to right: Ford Jr., David, Bruce, Ford Sr., Victor
Front from left to right: Giovanna, Sylvia, Benny

Author's Note

As I was nearing the end of writing my mother's story, I borrowed several of her old photographs. My intent was to scan them for the book and return them to her. Among those photographs was the one and only known image of her mother, Camilla, taken shortly before her death, and another of my mother, her father, and her brother Enrico together. Unfortunately, only ten days after borrowing those photographs, the Mississippi Gulf Coast was devastated by Hurricane Katrina. I was among the unfortunate people who lost their home. Those two photographs had been left behind in our hurry to escape the storm.

Although my husband and I had thirty-seven years of memories in our home, I spent many sleepless nights mourning and feeling guilty over the loss of those two photographs. It is remarkable that of all the many possessions I could have saved by taking them with me when I left my house, the manuscript of my mother's story was one of the few things I put in my car.

I am grateful to be able to share her story with the world.

978-0-595-39981-9
0-595-39981-9

Printed in the United States
97134LV00004B/139/A